Identifying, Assessing, and Treating Dyslexia at School

Developmental Psychopathology at School

Series Editors:

Stephen E. Brock, *California State University, Sacramento, CA, USA*
Shane R. Jimerson, *University of California, Santa Barbara, CA, USA*

Catherine Christo • John M. Davis
Stephen E. Brock

Identifying, Assessing, and Treating Dyslexia at School

 Springer

Catherine Christo
California State University, Sacramento
Department of Special Education,
Rehabilitation School Psychology,
& Deaf Studies
6000 J Street
Sacramento CA 95819-6079
USA
christo@csus.edu

John M. Davis
California State University,
East Bay
25800 Carlos Bee Blvd.
Hayward CA 94542-3095
USA
jack.davis@csueastbay.edu

Stephen E. Brock
California State University, Sacramento
Department of Special Education,
Rehabilitation School Psychology,
& Deaf Studies
6000 J Street
Sacramento CA 95819-6079
USA
brock@csus.edu

ISBN: 978-0-387-88599-5   e-ISBN: 978-0-387-88600-8
DOI: 10.1007/978-0-387-88600-8

Library of Congress Control Number: 2008942044

Printed on acid-free paper

springer.com

This book is dedicated to those children, families, and educational professionals who overcome the challenges associated with dyslexia.
We hope that this book contributes to the well-being of both students and professionals who deal with this learning challenge.

And to...
the memory of my mother, Doris Maxine Jenkins Fuller. May all my deeds honor her memory.

– CC

... the ones I love.

– JD

Christine who inspires me and reminds me of the importance of my efforts.

– SEB

Acknowledgments

As with any project of this magnitude, we believe it important to acknowledge the contributions of the individuals who have influenced our efforts. First, the authors are grateful for the collaboration with colleagues. Dr. Christo would like to particularly acknowledge Jack Davis for all the wonderful conversations about reading that serve to continually enlighten her and inspire her interest in the topic and those students who struggle with learning to read. Dr. Davis would like to give special thanks to all his friends and colleagues at the Raskob Institute for helping him learn what dyslexia is all about. He would like to give an extra special thanks to Mrs. Helen Nelson who managed to grind this information into his "semiresistant" brain. Dr. Brock would like to acknowledge Catherine Christo for her years of rewarding collaboration and helpful consultations regarding children with reading disabilities and Jack Davis for his mentorship. Finally, we collectively acknowledge the many scholars who have contributed to the science that provides the foundation for the information presented in this book; previous and future scholarship is essential to continue to advance our understanding of the multifaceted influences and interventions associated with dyslexia. We would like to particularly acknowledge Carl Spring for sparking our interest with his pioneering work in the field of reading disabilities.

Contents

Chapter 1
Introduction and Overview

If the 1990s were considered the decade of the brain (Bush, 1990), the second half of the 20th century and the first decade of the 21st should be considered the era of reading research. During this time, a plethora of studies have identified how children learn to read. Education professionals now have a much greater understanding of reading development from developmental, neuropsychological, and instructional viewpoints. The results of this research have informed instruction for regularly progressing readers and provided much greater understanding of why reading may not develop along the expected trajectory for some readers. This information has not only increased our understanding of the reading process, but has also been informative for the identification of characteristics that put children "at risk" for reading failure and for the development of instructional interventions that promote reading success for struggling readers. This chapter begins with a review of why school professionals should read this book, and then defines dyslexia, answers common questions about dyslexia, and examines this disorder from the context of special education eligibility.

Why School Professionals Should Read This Book

Clearly, school professionals should be especially attentive to ensuring that all students learn how to read. The following facts illustrate the consequences of reading disabilities or dyslexia. Specifically, the paragraphs that follow describe how reading is essential to academic success and adult outcomes, is associated with delinquency, and is the most common learning disability referral. Moreover, failure to identify and address dyslexia early on can have a cumulative effect. This reality is especially disturbing given the fact that much progress has been made in the early identification of dyslexia and in the development of interventions that successfully address reading disabilities. Finally, this introduction also suggests that school professionals should be interested in this book given that there have been recent changes in how to most effectively respond to the needs of children at risk for dyslexia.

C. Christo et al., *Identifying, Assessing, and Treating Dyslexia at School,*
DOI: 10.1007/978-0-387-88600-8_1, © Springer Science+Business Media, LLC 2009

School Success and Adult Outcomes

Becoming a competent reader is essential to school and occupational success. Without adequate reading skills, students are limited in both academic and employment prospects (National Endowment for the Arts, 2004). Reading is a foundational skill that is critical in acquiring content knowledge in academic areas such as science and social studies. Students with poor reading skills are at increased risk of dropping out of school (Frieden, 2004). Additionally, adults with dyslexia and other learning disabilities face greater difficulties in many aspects of adult life such as relationships and health (Mellard & Woods, 2007).

Association with Juvenile Delinquency

Further highlighting the need for educators to be better informed about reading disabilities is the relationship between dyslexia and youth who have had trouble with the law. Specifically, dyslexia has been documented to be more prevalent among adjudicated youth than in the general population. For example, Shelley-Tremblay, O'Brien, and Langhinrichsen-Rohling (2007) report that though prevalence rates vary all "... indicate that the rate of reading disabilities among juvenile delinquents is significantly higher than rates of reading disabilities among the general school-aged population" (p. 381). O'Brien, Langhinrichsen-Rohling, and Shelley-Tremblay (2007) found that 34% of incarcerated youth had reading problems; while Finn, Stott, and Zarichny (1988) reported that 43% of the adjudicated youth were two or more grade levels behind in reading. Incarcerated youth with reading problems are also found to have higher recidivism rates than those with adequate reading skills (Archwamety & Katslyannia, 2000).

The Most Common Learning Disability Referral

Reading problems are the predominate concern for children identified as having learning disabilities. They have been estimated to account for at least 80% of the referrals for learning disability evaluation (Lyon et al., 2001). Furthermore, the President's Commission on Excellence in Special Education (U.S. Department of Education, 2002) reports that over half the students receiving special education services had reading problems.

Importance of Early Identification and Intervention

Much progress has been made in early identification of children who are at risk for reading difficulties (Badian, 2000; Blachman et al., 2004; Foorman, Breier, & Fletcher, 2003; Shaywitz, 2003; Shaywitz & Shaywitz, 2004; Uhry & Clark, 2004).

This has led to the development of measures that are useful in identifying children who exhibit risk factors for reading difficulties (Al Otaiba & Fuchs, 2002, 2006; Davis, Lindo, & Compton, 2007; Foorman, 2003; Schatschneider & Torgesen, 2004; Vaughn & Fuchs, 2003).

Along with studies designed to identify risk factors, there has been a considerable amount of research regarding the benefits of early interventions and the difficulties students face when they are not provided with these services (Torgesen, 2002b). The majority of children (around 70%) who are poor readers in the primary grades continue to read poorly (McCardle, Scarborough, & Catts, 2001; Scarborough, 1998a, 1998b). In a landmark study, Juel and Leavell (1988) followed children's reading development during the primary grades and found that children who were poor readers in first grade remained poor readers in fourth grade, too. Stanovich (1986) used the term "Matthew effect" to describe the downward trajectory that poor readers experience in relation to normally developing peers if they do not receive adequate intervention. He described a trajectory wherein the gap between good and poor readers increases over time. Scarborough and Parker (2003) found that the gap did not necessarily increase in terms of standard scores, but that poor readers remained the same distance behind good readers. Other authors have also noted the virtual impossibility for poor readers to catch up if their reading trajectory is not changed within the first few years of schooling (Catts, Hogan, & Fey, 2003; Torgesen et al., 2001).

Conversely, the benefits of early intervention have been well documented (Foorman, 2003). For example, Denton and Mathes (2003) note that early intervention can be powerful in bolstering later student achievement. Torgesen (2002a, 2002b, 2004) has also demonstrated the positive impact of early intervention. Good classroom-level interventions are estimated to reduce the number of at-risk readers from 25% of the population to 6%. Further, more intensive, supplemental interventions can reduce the number of struggling readers to 3–4% (Foorman). In addition, recent research has demonstrated that brain functioning, observed through imaging studies of struggling readers, can be changed to more closely resembling typically developing readers following intervention (Shaywitz & Shaywitz, 2004; Simos et al., 2007). Achievement data accumulated through the *Reading First* program demonstrate improvements in reading for nearly every grade and subgroup (e.g., Hispanic, African American, disabled, English language learners, and economically disadvantaged; U.S. Department of Education, 2007).

Changes in How School Professionals Respond to Dyslexia

As a result of findings reflecting the effectiveness of early intervention, there has been a recent call for more efficient models for providing these interventions (Mellard & Johnson, 2008). While the value of early intervention for reading problems has been clearly established, many existing systems are not designed to provide sufficient intervention services to children until they are beyond the early primary years and are exhibiting more substantial academic deficits.

   The cited research findings have also led to reconsideration of how special education eligibility is determined and whether only students deemed eligible for special education should receive the services needed to increase their likelihood of academic success. This has resulted in an approach to intervention and eligibility considerations, which relies on student response to intervention (RTI) for determining who is in greatest need of intervention services. RTI approaches have as key elements early intervention with research-based instructional programs and frequent monitoring of student progress. Such approaches hold promise for significantly reducing the number of children who will have ongoing reading problems.

   However, even when implementing the most effective interventions there are still students who will struggle with learning to read. Characteristics of children less likely to respond to interventions have been identified (Fawcett & Nicolson, 2000; Muter, 1994). They include deficits in phonological awareness (Adams, 1990; Shaywitz, 2003; Torgesen, Wagner, Rashotte, Burgess, & Hecht, 1997), rapid naming (Lovett, Steinback, & Fritjers, 2000; Spring & Davis, 1988; Spring & Farmer, 1975; Wolf, 1991; Wolf, Bowers, & Biddle, 2000), and vocabulary (Al Otaiba & Fuchs, 2006). Methods of screening that operationalize these characteristics will be discussed further in Chap. 4.

Defining Dyslexia

To better understand the subject of this book and to set the stage for the chapters that follow, the following section reviews both the history of dyslexia and the current conceptualization of this developmental psychopathology.

History

Beaton (2004) provides a brief discussion of the first appearance of the term *dyslexia* as well as the condition that is currently associated with this term. According to Beaton, Sir Henry Broadbent was the first to mention this disorder in 1872, when he described patients who had lost the ability to read following brain injury. However, perhaps the most well-known early researcher on dyslexia was James Hinshelwood who published a series of papers describing cases of what was called "word and letter blindness." Hinshelwood went on to report on a family within which were found several cases of such "word blindness."

   The first English language scholarly reference to what we now refer to as dyslexia was published in the *British Medical Journal* by Dr. W. Pringle Morgan in 1896. One of the major difficulties with this original conceptualization was its assertion that dyslexia was caused primarily by a vision or a visual processing problem.

Morgan's perspective was the most prevalent until Orton's (1928) work, which introduced the concept of *strephosymbolia*, or simply put – problems with reversing letters and words. He proposed that there was a relationship between cerebral dominance and reading, which opened the door to viewing reading problems as due to more than just visual processing. Researchers such as Johnson and Myklebust (1967); Satz, Raredin, and Ross (1971); Witelson (1976); and Witelson and Rabinovitch (1972) continued this research and began to publish articles addressing right-hemisphere/spatial processing issues and left-hemisphere/linguistic deficits as possible causes of dyslexia. More recently, Liberman and Liberman's groundbreaking work at the Haskins Lab helped to identify difficulties in phonological processing as a root cause of reading problems (Liberman, 1999; Liberman, Shankweiler, Liberman, Fowler, & Fisher, 1977; Shankweiler et al., 1995). The presence of phonological processing problems in poor readers has been replicated in numerous studies (Fletcher, Lyon, Fuchs, & Barnes, 2007) and is now a well-established element of current conceptualizations of dyslexia.

Current Conceptualizations

The most frequently cited definition of dyslexia was developed by a working group of the International Dyslexia Association (IDA; Lyon, Shaywitz, & Shaywitz, 2003). This definition reads as follows:

> "Dyslexia is a specific learning disability that is neurobiological in origin. It is characterized by difficulties with accurate and/or fluent word recognition and by poor spelling and decoding abilities. These difficulties typically result from a deficit in the phonological component of language that is often unexpected in relation to other cognitive abilities and the provision of effective classroom instruction. Secondary consequences may include problems in reading comprehension and reduced reading experience that can impede growth of vocabulary and background knowledge." (p. 2)

There are several key points in this definition. First is the statement that dyslexia is of *neurobiological origin*. This statement indicates that to be considered dyslexia the reading difficulty must not be attributable to external environmental causes, such as poor instruction, and that the difficulty lies somewhere within the individual.

Second, the definition is very clear that dyslexia is related to problems at the word level (single word decoding) and not primarily an issue of understanding what was read (Vellutino, Fletcher, Snowling, & Scanlon, 2004). According to Fletcher et al. (2007) "word level reading disability (WLRD) is synonymous with 'dyslexia'" (p. 85). The role of phonological processing is also highlighted in this definition. As noted earlier, difficulties in phonological processing have been identified by numerous researchers as a central feature of reading disabilities and problems with reading development. Further discussion of phonological processing and its role in reading development will be provided in Chap. 2.

Third, the difficulties in reading are unexpected. Within this definition, dyslexia would not apply to students whose cognitive abilities were significantly below their age peers, or those who had not received adequate instruction in reading.

Finally, the definition notes that problems in single word decoding can lead to reading comprehension problems, and to limited growth in vocabulary and background knowledge. If children are not able to decode words effortlessly and automatically, they will have fewer resources to use in constructing meaning from text. In addition, an inability to correctly identify words along with slow and labored reading will impede comprehension. The effects of limited reading on vocabulary development and other academic skills have been described by Cunningham and Stanovich (1999).

Similar to the IDA definition, the National Institutes of Health's (National Institutes of Health & Development, 2007) definition of dyslexia emphasizes problems with word recognition and notes that individuals with this disability may have poor spelling, handwriting, and reading comprehension. The NIH definition is as follows:

> "Reading Disability is a reading and language-based learning disability, also commonly called dyslexia. For most children with learning disabilities receiving special education services, the primary area of difficulty is reading. People with reading disabilities often have problems recognizing words that they already know. They may also be poor spellers and may have problems with decoding skills. Other symptoms may include trouble with handwriting and problems understanding what they read. About 15 percent to 20 percent of people in the United States have a language-based disability, and of those, most have dyslexia." (¶ 8)

Another commonly referenced conceptualization of dyslexia is offered within the *Diagnostic and Statistical Manual of Mental Disorders* (4th Edition, Text Rev.; DSM-IV; American Psychiatric Association [APA], 2000), which places "Reading Disorder" within the class of "Disorders Commonly Diagnosed in Infancy, Childhood or Adolescence" (pp. 39–134) and is one of four Learning Disorders (with the others being Mathematics Disorder, Disorder of Written Expression, and Learning Disorder Not Otherwise Specified [NOS]). Within the description of this learning disorder, "dyslexia" is noted as a term that can also be used for "Reading Disorder" (pp. 51–52). The *DSM-IV-TR* description also notes that oral reading of persons with dyslexia "is characterized by distortions, substitutions or omissions" (p. 52). Problems in fluency are also highlighted in the *DSM-IV-TR* description: "both oral and silent reading are characterized by slowness and errors in comprehension" (p. 52). This description of the reading of individuals with Reading Disorder highlights similar difficulties in word-level identification, fluency, and comprehension included in the definition of dyslexia put forth by the IDA (Lyon et al., 2003). Further discussion of dyslexia criteria will be explored in Chap. 5, which addresses the topic of diagnosis. Table 1.1 provides a summary of the components of each of the definitions of dyslexia discussed here.

Table 1.1 Comparisons of dyslexia definition elements

Diagnostic element	Definition source		
	International Dyslexia Association (Lyon et al., 2003)	Diagnostic and Statistical Manual IV TR (APA, 2000)	National Institutes of Health (2007)
Etiology	Neurobiological Phonological process- ing skill insufficient	Not addressed	Neurological Phonological component of language deficit
Behavioral marker	Difficulties with single word decoding	Reading accuracy, speed, or compre- hension	Difficulties with accurate and/or fluent word recognition
Comparison of reading diffi- culties to other abilities	Unexpected relative to age, other cog- nitive academic abilities, and the provision of effec- tive instruction	Accuracy, speed, or comprehension substantially below age, intelligence, and age-appropriate education	Unexpected relative to other cognitive abilities and the provision of effective classroom instruction
Other conse- quences	Problems in reading comprehension and reduced reading experience	Oral and silent reading characterized by slowness and com- prehension errors	Problems in reading comprehension and reduced reading experience Impeded growth of vocabulary and back- ground knowledge

Common Questions About Dyslexia

Two questions are frequently asked about dyslexia. The first is whether dyslexia is simply the low end of the reading skill continuum, and the second is whether there are different "types" of dyslexia.

Is Dyslexia Just the Low End of the Reading Skill Continuum?

An important issue in defining dyslexia is whether dyslexia represents a unique disorder or the lower end of a continuum of reading skill. When dyslexia is defined on the basis of discrepancies between IQ and reading achievement, arguments against dyslexia being a valid clinical entity include (a) difficulty in differentiating between poor readers with low and high IQs (Shaywitz, Escobar, Shaywitz, Fletcher, & Makuch, 1992; Stanovich, 1993), (b) similar deficits in the key area of phonological processing (Fletcher & Shaywitz, 1994; Stanovich & Siegel, 1994), and (c) similar response to reading intervention programs (Felton, 1992). Thus, if dyslexia is conceptualized as problems in word recognition that have as their proximal cause difficulties in certain aspects of phonological processing, "garden variety" poor readers (Gough & Tunmer, 1986) cannot be distinguished from students with dyslexia on the basis of IQ and achievement discrepancies. Their reading problems, their underlying deficits, and their RTI are not sufficiently different to warrant categorization.

However, separate from the questions of IQ and reading achievement discrepancies, there is something unique about readers who struggle with basic word recognition. Specifically, there is substantial evidence for a unique phonological processing deficit defining dyslexic readers (which will be addressed further in Chap. 2). Performance on phonological processing tasks distinguishes good and poor readers from an early age, and is predictive of students who will struggle with the development of basic reading skills (the use of such tasks to predict who is at risk for reading difficulties will be addressed further in Chap. 4). In addition, interventions targeting phonological processing have been shown to be powerful remediation approaches. Such strong evidence of a clearly defined processing deficit linked to reading problems gives credence to the conceptualization of dyslexia as a unique disorder and not simply the lower end of the reading skill continuum.

In addition to the behavioral manifestations of a phonological processing deficit, neuroimaging studies have demonstrated functional differences in the brains of those identified as having dyslexia and those identified as average readers. These deficits are seen in beginning readers, can predict who will readily respond to intervention in dyslexic readers, and are linked to successful interventions (Shaywitz & Shaywitz, 2004; Simos et al., 2006). Coupled with the evidence of phonological processing differences, the identification of a "neural signature" of dyslexia presents a strong argument for dyslexia as a unique disorder.

Finally, genetic research also provides support for dyslexia as a unique disorder. Pennington and Olson (2005) report on a series of twin studies exploring the relationships among genetics, environment, and different aspects of reading skill as well as cognitive processes linked to reading development. These studies have provided evidence of the heritability of dyslexia as well as suggest what specific genes may be linked to reading difficulties.

In sum, the evidence appears to support the conceptualization of dyslexia as a disorder that is characterized by unique processing issues that are identifiable in those at risk for dyslexia and those whose reading development has lagged because of specific processing problems. At the same time, it is also important to acknowledge that multiple factors will affect whether a student learns to read and can either amplify or minimize impacts due to processing deficits. Hence, two children who have the same deficits in phonological processing may have different outcomes, dependent on factors such as language skills, environment, and instruction. Educators should be alert to the multiple factors that impact reading outcomes for individual children. Mitigating the impact of disruptive factors and fostering supportive factors are key strategies in designing effective interventions.

Are There Different Types of Dyslexia?

One differentiation made among individuals with dyslexia is between acquired and developmental dyslexia (Beaton, 2004). Acquired dyslexia refers to dyslexia that occurs after a person has learned how to read. Such dyslexia is usually the result of brain trauma impacting a particular aspect of reading. Developmental dyslexia, in contrast, refers to reading problems that arise during the development of reading skills. In addition to these two types of dyslexia, there are two primary subtypes of acquired dyslexia, which are distinguished by problems with reading different kinds of words. Surface dyslexia refers to those individuals who are able to decode and read nonsense words accurately, but who read irregularly spelled words incorrectly using learned phonics rules to sound them out (e.g., reading "island" as "is land"). The other subtype of acquired dyslexia is phonological dyslexia, which is manifest as the ability to read real words, but an inability to decode nonsense words.

A more relevant distinction for this book concerns possible subtypes of developmental dyslexia. Various subtypes of developmental dyslexia have been proposed, and Table 1.2 provides descriptions of the proposed subtypes of developmental dyslexia. Coltheart (2005) distinguishes between two subtypes of dyslexia similar to the two types of acquired dyslexia described earlier. He relates these to two routes for word recognition (a) a sublexical route that uses decoding for word

Table 1.2 Proposed subtypes of developmental dyslexia

Proposed type	Description
Coltheart (2005)	
Phonological dyslexia	Sublexical impairment
	Can read known real words
	Cannot decode nonsense words
Surface dyslexia	Lexical impairment
	Can decode nonsense words and read phonetically
	Cannot read irregular words correctly
Spafford and Grosser (2005)	
Visual dysphonetic	Can read known real words
	Cannot decode nonsense words
Dyseidetic	Can decode nonsense words and read phonetically
	Cannot read irregular words correctly
Dysphonetic-Dyseidetic	Difficulties in both areas
Bowers (2001), Wolf (2001), Wolf and Bowers (1999)	
Phonological processing deficit	Do poorly on phonological processing tasks such as segmenting and blending
Rapid naming deficit	Do poorly on naming tasks requiring rapid retrieval of name codes for overlearned material
Double deficit	Have deficits in both (most impaired readers)

identification and (b) a lexical route that uses visual recognition of the word without the necessity of decoding. Children with impairment in the sublexical route will be able to read real words at a normal level, but will not be able to decode nonsense words. This impairment is labeled "phonological dyslexia." Children with impairment in the lexical route will display adequate decoding skills and be able to read real words that follow regular spelling patterns as well as nonsense words; they will struggle with reading real words that do not follow a regular spelling pattern. These children are considered to have surface dyslexia. Coltheart cites various case studies as evidence of these two different types of developmental dyslexia.

Spafford and Grosser (2005) propose three different subtypes of dyslexia. The first type is called "visual dysphonetic" and is used to classify those individuals who, similar to Coltheart's (2005) phonological dyslexics, struggle with decoding, but perform adequately with irregularly spelled real words. The second type are labeled "dyseidetic" and are similar to surface dyslexics described by Coltheart in that these individuals are able to decode words, but have trouble with reading or spelling irregularly spelled real words. The third type is a combined "dysphonetic-dyseidetic" type, which manifests as deficits in both areas.

Another approach to subtyping has been put forth by Wolf and Bowers (Bowers, 2001; Wolf, 2001; Wolf & Bowers, 1999). This framework rests in the identification of two cognitive processes related to early reading problems: phonological processing and rapid automatic naming (RAN). Wolf and Bowers have proposed that there are three types of dyslexic readers: those with either a phonological or a rapid naming deficit and those with both. They report that individuals with deficits in both areas (double deficit) are the most impaired.

Morris and Shaywitz (1998) administered a variety of cognitive and academic tests to a large sample of children identified as having a reading disability. Seven different subtypes of reading disability were identified. However, readers in six of the seven types displayed weaknesses in measures of phonological awareness. Morris and colleagues concluded that the results supported a view of reading disability that "postulated a core problem in the development of phonological awareness skills" (p. 368). However, they further state that the subtypes provide evidence of variability across other domains that affect reading development and that this variability may be beneficial for intervention design. Consequently, this model may prove useful to practitioners in psychoeducational evaluations and in providing information relevant to the development of interventions.

Dyslexia and Special Education Eligibility

In the *Individuals with Disabilities Education Improvement Act* (IDEIA, 2004), dyslexia is specifically identified within the category of "specific learning disability." The definition of a specific learning disability (SLD) is found in Section 300.8 (c)(10) of the final regulations (U.S. Department of Education, 2006) and reads as follows:

"(10) Specific learning disability.

(i) General. Specific learning disability means a disorder in one or more of the basic psychological processes involved in understanding or in using language, spoken or written, that may manifest itself in the imperfect ability to listen, think, speak, read, write, spell, or to do mathematical calculations, including conditions such as perceptual disabilities, brain injury, minimal brain dysfunction, dyslexia, and developmental aphasia.

(ii) Disorders not included. Specific learning disability does not include learning problems that are primarily the result of visual, hearing, or motor disabilities, of mental retardation, of emotional disturbance, or of environmental, cultural, or economic disadvantage." [Section 300.8 (c)(10) of the IDEIA Code of Federal Regulations (CFR), p. 46551]

Thus, for special education purposes, a student with dyslexia would be considered a student with a specific learning disability. Determining that a student with dyslexia meets the criteria for special education eligibility requires that the procedures for determining the presence of an SLD be followed. Key points in the definition of SLD include the presence of a disorder in a basic psychological process, problems in academic subjects, and the exclusion of other disabling conditions.

Two significant changes in eligibility requirements are found in *IDEIA, 2004* (U.S. Department of Education, 2006). The first was the inclusion of a clause specifically stating that states could not require Local Education Agencies (LEA) to find a significant discrepancy between ability and achievement prior to determining eligibility for special education. Following are the regulations developed by the U.S. Department of Education that address this component of *IDEIA*:

(a) "General. A State must adopt, consistent with § 300.309, criteria for determining whether a child has a specific learning disability as defined in § 300.8. In addition, the criteria adopted by the State--;

(1) Must not require the use of a severe discrepancy between intellectual ability and achievement for determining whether a child has a specific learning disability, as defined in § 300.8(c)(10);

(2) Must permit the use of a process based on the child's response to scientific, research-based intervention; and

(3) May permit the use of other alternative research-based procedures for determining whether a child has a specific learning disability, as defined in § 300.8(c)(10)."

The second was the inclusion of a clause highlighting the importance of students receiving appropriate instruction in reading and of schools monitoring student progress in reading and sharing that information with parents. Section 300.306, determination of eligibility, includes the following:

(b) "Special rule for eligibility determination. A child must not be determined to be a child with a disability under this part--

(1) If the determinant factor for that determination is--

(i) Lack of appropriate instruction in reading, including the essential components of reading instruction (as defined in Section 1208(3) of the ESEA)."

This section of the regulations refers back to the essential components of reading outlined in the most recent reauthorization of the *Elementary and Secondary Education Act*, known as *No Child Left Behind* (NCLB). These include the use of scientific research-based methods of reading instruction that are aligned with the findings of the National Reading Panel (2000). The inclusion of this special rule is meant to assure that students who receive special education services are truly disabled and not merely "casualties" of poor instruction. The importance of appropriate instruction is further stressed in Section 300.309, which further addresses determining the existence of a specific learning disability.

> (c) "To ensure that underachievement in a child suspected of having a specific learning disability is not due to lack of appropriate instruction in reading or math, the group must consider, as part of the evaluation described in §§ 300.304 through 300.306--
>
> > (1) Data that demonstrate that prior to, or as a part of, the referral process, the child was provided appropriate instruction in regular education settings, delivered by qualified personnel; and
> >
> > (2) Data-based documentation of repeated assessments of achievement at reasonable intervals, reflecting formal assessment of student progress during instruction, which was provided to the child's parents."

This section also stresses the importance of monitoring student progress in reading and sharing that information with parents. These excerpts from *IDEIA* regulations reflect the findings of a number of commissions and panels that addressed needs in special education prior to the reauthorization of *IDEIA*. These included the National Research Council report on minority over-representation in special education (Donovan & Cross, 2002); a report entitled *Rethinking Special Education* by the Fordham Foundation and the Progressive Policy Institute (Finn, Rotherman, & Hokanson, 2001); proceedings of the Learning Disabilities Summit by the US Office of Special Education Programs (Bradley, Danielson, & Hallahan, 2002); and the report of the President's Commission on Excellence in Special Education (2002). The emphasis placed on appropriate instruction and monitoring of student progress also reflects important components of *NCLB*, which highlighted sound instructional methods and the necessity of providing highly qualified teachers.

Purpose and Plan of the Book

The purpose of this book is to provide education professionals with an understanding of dyslexia that includes causes, prevalence, approaches to evaluation, and research-based interventions. This book is expected to serve as a valuable resource in identifying, understanding, and addressing the needs of students with dyslexia. It is important for school psychologists and other education professionals to understand dyslexia and how it differs from other reading problems as this is necessary to eligibility considerations and informative to instructional planning.

Chapter 2 provides an overview of the possible causes of dyslexia, and Chap. 3 discusses the prevalence of dyslexia and commonly co-occurring disorders. Of critical importance is that education professionals recognize the early reading difficulties that children exhibit that may put them at risk of developing dyslexia. In this way, it may be possible to provide the early intervention services that will reduce the need for special education placements. Chapter 4 provides information related to case finding and screening, while Chaps. 5 and 6 address diagnosis, special education eligibility decisions, and intervention-focused assessment. More specifically, Chap. 5 addresses clinical diagnosis from the point of *DSM-IV-TR* criteria, whereas Chap. 6 addresses evaluation for special education eligibility purposes. With *IDEIA* (2004), the options for determining the presence of a specific learning disability (which is where dyslexia falls) have expanded beyond the traditional ability/achievement discrepancy model that has been key to *DSM-IV-TR* diagnosis. Therefore, the data sufficient for a *DSM-IV-TR* diagnosis of reading disorder will not be sufficient for special education eligibility considerations. These issues will be more thoroughly addressed in Chaps. 5 and 6. It is also important for education professionals to understand that dyslexia is a lifelong condition, and though students may compensate well given early intervention and necessary supports, the condition will remain (Mellard & Woods, 2007). Chapter 7 describes interventions and instructional approaches that have proven successful in serving the needs of students with dyslexia throughout their schooling.

Chapter 2
Causes

This chapter explores three primary issues. First, it will consider how theories addressing the etiology of dyslexia have changed over time. Next, it will examine current theories regarding what causes dyslexia. Finally, the chapter concludes with a review of empirical investigations addressing the genetic, neurobiological, and environmental causes of dyslexia.

Changes in Perspective of the Etiology of Dyslexia

As discussed in Chap. 1, the original conceptualizations (originally termed "word blindness") viewed dyslexia as being caused primarily by a vision or a visual processing problem. It was not until Liberman, Shankweiler, Orlando, Harris, and Bell-Beitz's (1971) research on Orton's (1928) classic "symptoms" of dyslexia, b and d reversals, and reading words backward that linguistic processes were considered most important. Liberman et al. found that Orton's classic symptoms were actually much more a normal developmental variation rather than a set of specific symptoms or predictors of dyslexia. This allowed the field to begin to delve more deeply into the linguistic processes related to dyslexia, which has led to the current dominant understanding regarding the causes of dyslexia discussed later.

In Vellutino's (1979) classic *Dyslexia: Theory and Research*, most of the available research of the time was reviewed. He and others helped to launch what has become a much more productive era of focusing on linguistic or language processing as being central to the etiology of dyslexia. Phonological processing, rather than visual processing, has been found to be a more relevant predictor for and *causative* of dyslexia. Perhaps even more important, it has become the most important and successful target of interventions. However, in our interactions with parents and school personnel, we find it notable that many parents, and even some educators, persist in believing that dyslexia is primarily a visual processing problem.

From research conducted during the 1970s and 1980s, phonological processing has come to be viewed as a significant, if not the most significant, variable contributing to our understanding of the etiology of dyslexia (Bradley & Bryant, 1983; Calfee, Lindamood, & Lindamood, 1973; Liberman & Shankweiler, 1985;

Vellutino, 1979). The collective empirical data were so persuasive that in 1987 the Federal Government was convinced to pursue a large-scale, multisite study. At that time, the National Institute of Child Health and Development (NICHD), a branch of the National Institutes of Health (NIH), issued a request for proposals to establish research centers to further this knowledge base. This national research project was headed by G. Reid Lyon who had facilitated the research programs of many outstanding reading researchers and neuroscientists over those decades. This research forms the foundation for contemporary conceptualizations of dyslexia.

Current Theoretical Views on the Etiology of Dyslexia

This section reviews four primary areas of research and theory on dyslexia. First, it reviews two theories that reflect a re-emergence of the idea that visual processing is central to dyslexia. Next, this section examines a conceptualization based on efficient temporal processing. The third approach to be reviewed is the phonological core deficit model, which is the best-supported etiological explanation for dyslexia. Finally, this section examines variations on the phonological core deficit, which include dual coding approaches and multiple subtype approaches. These approaches in some ways try to bring together aspects of most of the previously discussed theories.

Visual Processing Approaches

Two primary schools of thought continue to focus on visual systems as related to reading and dyslexia. The older of the two theories (Buswell, 1922) has shown that reading skill influences eye movements. Rayner (1978, 1998) has expanded on this and suggested that at least some reading problems are caused by tracking issues. Tracking is defined as when the eyes move across the page of print attempting to extract meaning. Although the eyes of the reader may appear to be gliding across a page, they are actually engaging in fixations (i.e., where the eye stops for 200–250 ms and *takes in* information) and saccades (i.e., where the eye moves for about 20–40 ms moving from the next stimuli to the subsequent one, but *is not* taking in information). Thus, students who have problems with this type of eye movement are believed to be at risk for reading problems.

There has been an ongoing debate about whether tracking issues cause reading problems or whether reading problems cause tracking issues. One position on this espoused by Eden, Stein, Wood, and Wood (1994) has identified two ways in which eye movement difficulties can create problems. First, they propose that children with reading problems may have difficulties with fixation stability at the end of a fixation pause when reading. Second, poor readers may have vergence difficulties that can interfere with binocular vision and impede reading. Berninger and Richards

(2002) suggest that increasing print size for the former and eye patching for the latter could be helpful.

More controversy exists around the vision tracking and other "visual" exercises that are sometimes proposed as alternative interventions for reading problems. A joint statement by the American Academy of Pediatrics, American Academy of Ophthalmology, and American Association for Pediatric Ophthalmology and Strabismus (1998) stated that:

> Eye defects, subtle or severe, do not cause the patient to experience reversal of letters, words, or numbers. No scientific evidence supports claims that the academic abilities of children with learning disabilities can be improved with treatments that are based on (1) visual training, including muscle exercises, ocular pursuit, tracking exercises, or "training" glasses (with or without bifocals or prisms); (2) neurological organizational training (laterality training, crawling, balance board, perceptual training); or (3) colored lenses. These more controversial methods of treatment may give parents and teachers a false sense of security that a child's reading difficulties are being addressed, which may delay proper instruction or remediation. The expense of these methods is unwarranted, and they cannot be substituted for appropriate educational measures. Claims of improved reading and learning after visual training, neurologic organization training, or use of colored lenses are almost always based on poorly controlled studies that typically rely on anecdotal information. These methods are without scientific validation. Their reported benefits can be explained by the traditional educational remedial techniques with which they are usually combined." (p. 1217)

The second theory based on visual processing has to do with the efficiency of the magnocellular system. This vision system is associated with detecting motion sensitivity. Stein and colleagues (Stein & Talcott, 1999; Stein & Walsh, 1997; Talcott et al., 1998) contend that slow processing in this system can interfere with letter position information. Others (Eden et al., 1996) have begun to establish brain imaging evidence that poor readers experience during a deficit in this type of fast visual processing. Stein (2001) who proposes an integrated theory has also noted that motion sensitivity, which takes place in the magnocellular system, predicts orthographic skills. Thus, it is possible that as the research unfolds there may be convergence of the orthographic and the magnocellular views on the etiology of dyslexia.

Temporal Processing

In the same way that inefficient or slow processing in the visual system was explored, Tallel and colleagues (Tallal, 1980; Tallal, Miller, & Fitch, 1993; Temple et al., 2000) have pursued the notion that inefficient *temporal* processing is central to the etiology of dyslexia. This approach explains these difficulties as the brain's inability to perform tasks requiring the processing of brief stimuli in rapid temporal or sequential succession. This approach postulates that there is a causative link between the ability to process auditory input effectively and the ability to perceive phonemes. They do not deny that phonological processing is important, but postulate

that phonological processing difficulties are a symptom of this more basic underlying disorder. Studies have found that children with dyslexia do have difficulty
when having to differentiate between rapidly changing consonant–vowel (CV)
syllables when these are presented to them at what is considered a normal rate of
speech (Tallal et al., 1993, 1996).

Phonological Core Deficit

Given the available research, it is clear that most researchers and practitioners
consider phonological deficits as the core deficit of dyslexia/decoding problems
(Adams, 1990; Bradley & Bryant, 1983; Calfee et al., 1973; Catts, 1989; Liberman
& Shankweiler, 1985; Lyon, Shaywitz, & Shaywitz, 2003; Rosner, 1974; Wagner
& Torgesen, 1987). The volume of research on this topic is so convincing that many
have opined that it is difficult to imagine any research on dyslexia not referencing
the role of phonological awareness (Foorman, 2003; Uhry & Clark, 2004). So
what then is phonological awareness? Torgesen (1995) has defined it as:

> "A language skill that is critically important in learning to read … phonological awareness
> can be formally defined as sensitivity to, or explicit awareness of, the phonological struc-
> ture of words in one's language. When fully developed, it involves the ability to identify,
> think about, and manipulate the individual sounds in words." (p.4)

Thus, at this point, phonological processing is entrenched in the theory of what
causes dyslexia, and few would argue with its centrality to the disorder. However,
this does not mean that the case is closed. Currently, there remain other views
regarding the causes of reading problems that are worth reviewing.

Dual Subtype Approaches

There are a number of theorists and researchers who, although often recognizing
the import of phonological processing, also view phonology as too limiting a theory
to explain the varieties and vagaries of dyslexia. They have proposed additions to
the model, which they present as important in understanding dyslexia. The following discussion represents some of what the authors believe to be the more relevant
approaches.

Keith Stanovich and colleagues (Cunningham & Stanovich, 1998; Stanovich,
1988; Stanovich, West, & Harrison, 1995) have attempted to differentiate between
those who struggle with reading due to more environmental reasons or *developmental
delay* issues, as opposed to those that better fit into a *deficit* model, which they have
suggested may be more associated with greater genetic predispositions. In his
earlier work, Stanovich (1986, 1988) began to explore what he referred to as the
"Matthew effect" in reading, referring to the biblical Matthew where the rich got

richer and the poor got poorer; or how those who enter school with more skills more easily acquire and accrue greater benefit from instruction.

In a review of reading studies in the late 1980s, Stanovich (1986) summated that "the presently available evidence would appear to suggest the hypothesis that the 'garden variety' poor reader is characterized by a developmental lag; whereas the much rarer, dyslexic child displays a specific phonological deficit, in conjunction with compensatory use of other skills and knowledge sources" (p. 280). In his later research, he found that the "garden variety" children were often in part delayed due to less exposure to print, or the prekindergarten equivalent of less exposure to language and to being read to (Cunningham & Stanovich, 1998; Stanovich et al., 1995). Supporting this point of view is the literature exploring how most of the underprivileged children who enter kindergarten are already behind their middle class peers in language development (Lerner, 2003).

Another early dual subtype alternative was Dirk Bakker's *P-type* and *L-type* dyslexics (Bakker, 1979, 2006; Bakker, Licht, Kok, & Bouma, 1980). Bakker's position has been that early reading is primarily mediated by the right hemisphere. He suggests that in normal development as the demands of reading become more linguistically complex, reading shifts and becomes more mediated by left-hemisphere processes. However, some children continue to overuse right-hemisphere strategies instead of shifting strategies, which can hinder the development of left-hemisphere strategies. He referred to this type as a P-type dyslexic (*p* for perceptual) because this subtype tends to learn to read utilizing more visual-perceptual strategies. His L-type dyslexic (*l* for linguistic deficits) tends to demonstrate an over-reliance on linguistic and/or semantic strategies in their beginning stage of learning as well as continued reading development. It seems that neither subtype develops the neural networking that is necessary for fluent reading that Berninger and Richards (2002) describe when they state that "sound codes in speech play a fundamental role in the recoding of visual stimuli into language; these recoded stimuli are stored as orthographic word form representations" (p. 112). It is this development, which occurs with exposure and instruction, that allows for the development of reading fluency.

A third dual subtype model, more recently developed, has been focusing on phonological processing and what has been referred to as "rapid automatized naming" (RAN) by Denckla and Rudel (1976a, 1976b), or what Shaywitz (2003) has referred to as "phonological accessing efficiency." What has been postulated and fairly well supported by the research is that in addition to phonological issues, children with dyslexia also struggle with the ability to efficiently access overlearned information, like words, numbers, and letters (Bowers, Sunseth, & Golden, 1999; Bowers & Wolf, 1993; Wolf & Bowers, 1999). This inability to access information efficiently creates problems with reading, primarily sight words and reading fluency, which can secondarily impact reading comprehension. As Uhry and Clark (2004) have reported, "in our clinical practice, we find that being at least one, and usually two, standard deviations slower than peers on more than one RAN subtest is common for children with severe and enduring difficulty in acquiring speed in decoding" (p. 70). Over the years, this combination of deficits has been more commonly referred to as the "double deficit hypothesis" with some supporting research that having both deficits renders remediation a more difficult task (Lovett, Steinbach, & Fritjers, 2000).

Other researchers, however, have not found the double deficit to be as strongly associated with reading remediation success. For example, Ackerman (Ackerman & Dykman, 1993; Ackerman, Holloway, Youngdahl, & Dykman, 2001) found no additive effect of slow naming above and beyond phonological awareness. The "single deficit" children were equally as impacted as their "double deficit" peers in these studies. However, these studies were not remedial studies, but rather current condition studies, so it is possible that the "double deficit" children could be more difficult to remediate. Obviously, further research is needed.

Multiple Subtype Approaches

Probably the most common of the multiple subtypes suggests the need to account for phonological processing, rapid automatized naming, and orthographic processing in the understanding of dyslexia. Badian (2005) has been one of the researchers trying to develop this model, but clearly is not alone (Berninger, 1994; Manis, Doi, & Bhadha, 2000; Olson, Forsberg, & Wise, 1994; Roberts & Mather, 1997). The arguments for this position tend to come from two related yet different areas: research and clinical intervention.

Ackerman et al. (2001) argue that multiple regression analyses indicate that the double deficit theory still leaves unanswered questions as not all variance is explained after phonological processing and rapid naming are entered into the regression equation on basic reading measures. Thus, until we can explain as much variance as possible, we should continue to look for other contributing variables.

Roberts and Mather (1997) argue from a clinical perspective that it is likely that when different processes are *causing* the child's reading problems, different interventions will be needed to help solve or at least ameliorate those reading problems. Either way, Lachmann (2002) argues that it is the unstable encoding of the letters, or any orthographic information, that can create accessing difficulties. Furthermore, Lachmann believes that it is not that dyslexic children *see* reversals when these kinds of mistakes are evident, but that these reversals occur in memory and that it is the revisualizing of the orthographic elements that creates the difficulties.

Harkening back to the visual processing approaches, Stein, Talcott, and Witton's (2001) research has demonstrated a link between magnocellular dysfunction and the transposition of letters. Stein and his colleagues also found that motion sensitivity (magnocellular function) correlated with orthographic skills and spelling, and even accounted for unique variance after controlling for phonological skills in basic reading. It seems likely that research in this multiple subtype mode will continue. However, in the authors' opinion, the research base for intervention is strongest in the phonological core deficit and the temporal processing approaches.

Genetic, Neurobiological, and Environmental Contributions to the Understanding of Dyslexia

This section presents an overview of how the current knowledge base of genetic, neurobiological, and environmental factors further contributes to our understanding of dyslexia. Before proceeding, however, it is important to note that much of this research has come out of the NICHD multisite studies, based on the phonological core deficit model, so the current knowledge base focuses primarily on the genetics of phonological processing difficulties.

Genetics

Since reading is a relatively recent cultural advancement and does not even exist among all cultures, it is unlikely that we have evolved a "reading" gene. However, this does not mean that there are no genetic influences or predispositions that affect this skill. Over the last 50 years, there has been a great deal of advancement in this area, and the primary findings of this research are offered in Table 2.1. As far back as 1950 Hallgren, studying six families, found very significant correlations between reading problems and family membership. Studies like these were followed up by direct genotypic studies looking at dyslexia and learning disorders. For instance, Pennington, Bender, Puck, Salbenblatt, and Robinson (1982) found a higher rate of language and reading problems in boys and girls with an extra X chromosome (47, XXY and 47, XXX). A follow-up study using the few genetic markers available was made, and a linkage was found between dyslexia and chromosome 15 (Smith, Kimberling, Pennington, & Lubs, 1983).

Table 2.1 Current findings regarding the genetics of reading

Familiality and heritability are clearly documented and the influences operate similarly in males and females. Heritability estimates are 0.55 ± 0.22 depending on the measures used (Pennington & Olson, 2005)

Dyslexia is unlikely to be a "one gene" variant because of the evidence of multiple risk loci (Fisher & DeFries, 2002)

Chromosomes 6 and 15 have the most evidence of contributing to reading, although chromosomes 1, 2, 3, and 18 have also been implicated (Cardon et al., 1994; Grigorencko et al., 1997; Pennington & Olson, 2005)

The same genes linked to dyslexia are also linked to *normal* reading skills; hence, dyslexia would not be considered a *disease* model (Boada et al., 2002)

There is evidence of genetic comorbidity between AD/HD and dyslexia (Willcutt et al., 2000, 2002)

Genetic predispositions impact the multiple cognitive components of dyslexia as postulated in the multiple subtype model (Raskind et al., 2000)

Perhaps the most well-known research for these types of genetic studies is the Colorado Twin Study, started at the University of Colorado in 1978 by John DeFries (DeFries, Singer, Foch, & Letwitter, 1978), which continues today with ever-increasingly sophisticated approaches to the understanding of genetics, the analysis of genetic material, and data analysis techniques. Other labs are also involved. As understanding of the genetic influences on dyslexia expands, some studies are finding that there are different correlations between genes and the multiple subtype approach with contributions by rapid naming and orthographic coding as well as phonology (Davis et al., 2001; Grigorencko et al., 1997; Raskind, Hsu, Berninger, Thomson, & Wijsman, 2000).

Studies are also beginning to investigate whether there is a genetic predisposition to the comorbidity found with learning disorders and dyslexia. For instance, one interesting longitudinal study found that *future dyslexic* children did not differ from controls on measures of dysthymia before kindergarten. They did, however, have higher rates of AD/HD symptoms before kindergarten suggesting that the dysthymia was secondary to the beginning of reading difficulties, while AD/HD was comorbid with reading disorders (Willcutt, Pennnington, & DeFries, 2000). In a subsequent study, the research group found evidence on chromosome 6 for a shared genetic risk for both dyslexia and AD/HD (Willcutt et al., 2002).

Neurobiological Structures

A variety of approaches are used in attempts to determine which parts of the brain are most associated with reading and/or its disorders. Research has proceeded from early brain autopsy data to the different brain scanning technologies of today. Autopsy data were aided by the establishment of the "brain bank" in 1982 by the then Orton Dyslexia Society at the Harvard Medical Department of Neurology at Beth Israel Hospital in Boston. The most commonly used technologies in dyslexia research over the last 10–15 years have included a variety of increasingly sophisticated imaging techniques (e.g., Computer-Assisted Tomography, Magnetic Resonance Imaging). For interested readers, Berninger and Richards (2002) provide a very good overview of the different technologies.

It has been fairly well established that good child and adult readers use different parts of the brain than their dyslexic counterparts (Hoeft et al., 2006; Shaywitz et al., 2004; Voeller, 2004). The most established pattern of brain activities is that good readers of all ages activate the occipito-temporal areas in the back of the brain when reading. As Berninger and Richards (2002) have described, this is where the occipital cortex and the "phonological loop" develop their neural connections, which are then used for proficient/fluent reading, or, in other words, where the orthographic system gets recoded into the phonologic system. Dyslexic readers tend not to have developed this "fluency center" and instead tend to overutilize left frontal (Broca's Area, most often associated with phonologic processing) and right frontal (most often associated with visual memory and executive functions) areas of the brain. However, Price and McCrory (2005) have argued that because most of the studies that have documented this have only had same-age controls without reading-age controls, it is impossible to know whether the reading problems caused the brain patterns or vice versa. Newer studies, such as Hoeft et al., have addressed this issue and their work corroborates that of Berninger and Richards. Additional studies have found that when students with dyslexia receive appropriate evidence-based treatments not only do their reading scores improve, but also their brain activation profile becomes normal following the remedial training (Shaywitz et al.; Simos et al., 2002).

Environment

Even though the heritability of dyslexia is high, with as many as 23–65% of children who have a parent with dyslexia also having dyslexia (Shaywitz, 2003), clearly the relationship is not perfect. This means, as noted earlier, that though one can have a mild-to-significant propensity toward dyslexia, the environment can then serve to support or not support the development of basic skills. Stanovich's concept of "garden variety" readers (1986, 1988) suggests that one can have a low propensity toward dyslexia, but still have significant difficulty with reading due to early lack of exposure to language and print. It is also known that environmental factors can impact later language development as well as phonological development (Voeller, 2004), clarifying that these are not "either or" issues, but more of a "how much and how many" issues. As has been often stated, development is the interaction between maturation/genetics and environment, and both have to be accounted for.

Research such as the Connecticut Longitudinal Study (Shaywitz, 2003) also reveals that about 20% of children are "at risk" for reading problems and without appropriate intervention can develop significant difficulties. However, studies have found that with appropriate early intervention the numbers of students who go on to develop significant reading problems can be reduced. Research suggests that the 20% can be reduced to somewhere between 3 and 6% (Denton & Mathes, 2003; Torgesen et al., 1999).

Concluding Comments

Over the last 30 years, it has become clear that dyslexia is real. It has been defined, it can be diagnosed, and there are empirically supported interventions. Contemporary research suggests it is a neurobiological disorder that best fits a dimensional model, which is that dyslexia occurs along a continuum based on the number and the severity of symptoms. Currently, the phonological core deficit is the most supported model for understanding dyslexia, but the more recent multiple subtype models consisting of at least phonological processing, rapid naming, and orthographic processing will likely receive much more attention in the near future. Since estimates are that around 80% of students who are identified as learning disabled are likely to have a linguistic processing disorder such as dyslexia, it is incumbent on school professionals to understand the etiology of this disorder (Lyon et al., 2001).

Chapter 3
Prevalence and Associated Conditions

It is not possible to discuss the prevalence of dyslexia without first considering the overall reading competence of our nation's children. The National Assessment of Educational Progress (NAEP) is a federally directed project that evaluates key academic skills of children in 4th, 8th, and 12th grades. Test results yield both scale scores and a percentage of students who are considered to be at a basic, proficient, or advanced level in terms of mastering the content deemed appropriate for their grade level. The 2007 NAEP (Lee, Grigg, & Donahue, 2007) report found that only 33% of fourth-grade students were performing in reading at what would be considered a proficient level for their grade. Proficient readers "should be able to demonstrate an overall understanding of the text, providing inferential as well as literal information" (p. 20). This situation is more troublesome when considering that only 14% of Black fourth graders, 17% of Hispanic fourth graders, and 20% of American Indian fourth graders are performing at a proficient level in reading. When considering the percentage of children who are at a basic level, defined as "partial mastery of the knowledge and skills fundamental for proficient work at a given grade," (p. 2) the results are even more disturbing. Among all fourth graders tested, 33% had not attained a basic level. Again, the disaggregated scores paint a bleaker picture for students of minority backgrounds, with about half of Black, Hispanic, and American Indian fourth graders not attaining a basic level in reading. It is clear from these statistics that reading proficiency is a serious educational concern. As discussed in Chap. 1, a lack of basic reading skills creates significant impediments to academic and occupational success, and is associated with an increased risk for incarceration and other negative outcomes.

Do all these children lacking basic reading skills have dyslexia? Certainly, it seems unlikely that between 33 and 66% of fourth graders have a disability as severe as dyslexia. Referring to the IDA (Lyon, Shaywitz, & Shaywitz, 2003) definition of dyslexia presented in Chap. 1, as a definitional criterion it is quite possible that a majority of these children have "difficulties with single word decoding" as dyslexia is defined in the IDA definition, and clearly they will suffer secondary consequences as a result of their word level reading problems. However, it is unlikely that all these children have a disorder "that is neurobiological in origin" or that they have been provided with "effective classroom instruction," two other

C. Christo et al., *Identifying, Assessing, and Treating Dyslexia at School*,
DOI: 10.1007/978-0-387-88600-8_3, © Springer Science+Business Media, LLC 2009

elements in the IDA definition (p. 2). Indeed, for many of these children, their lack of progress in reading may be due to lack of effective classroom instruction and/ or early intervention. To better understand the "true" prevalence of dyslexia, it is helpful to look at the results of studies that have provided effective classroom instruction and early intervention for struggling readers, thus eliminating the factor of ineffective instruction as a cause of basic reading deficits.

Nonresponders

One way to think about the prevalence of dyslexia is to consider the percentage of children who continue to struggle with reading despite solid research-based instruction and intervention. Within current response-to-intervention (RTI) models, these children are often referred to as "nonresponders" (Al Otaiba & Fuchs, 2006; Torgesen, 2002a, 2002b). Various studies over the last 10 years indicate that with effective instruction and intervention in the early grades the percentage of students who continue to read below the average range can be reduced to between 2 and 6% of the school population (Denton & Mathes, 2003; Foorman, Breier, & Fletcher, 2003; Foorman, Francis, Fletcher, Schwartz, & Mehta, 1998; Foorman, Francis, & Shaywitz, 1997; Shaywitz, 2003). In a longitudinal study, Torgesen and colleagues (Torgesen et al., 2001; Torgesen, Wagner, & Rashotte, 1997) evaluated the fourth-grade reading skills of students who had received different reading interventions from kindergarten through second grade. They found that early, direct, explicit intervention in beginning stage of reading skills reduced the prevalence of reading disability to an extrapolated figure of about 2% of the population.

Many recent studies have focused on providing instruction and intervention within an RTI model that provides successively more intense levels of intervention subsequent to a student's response to less intense intervention. The foundation of such approaches is a high-quality, research-based, general education reading curriculum provided to all students. Those who are not making adequate progress within the general curriculum are provided with further support, either in the classroom or in supplemental tutoring. Such models have demonstrated reductions in the number of students displaying reading difficulties to between 2 and 8% of the total population (Mathes et al., 2005; McMaster, Fuchs, Fuchs, & Compton, 2005; O'Connor, Fulmer, Harty, & Bell, 2005; Vellutino, Scanlon, Small, & Fanuele, 2006). Fletcher, Lyon, Fuchs, and Barnes (2007) summarize data from prevention studies and highlight the finding that in intervention programs that layer classroom and tutorial interventions "the number of at-risk students appears to go below 2% in some studies" (p. 149).

Other figures on prevalence include those provided by the International Dyslexia Association (IDA) and the National Institutes of Child Health and Development (NICHD). According to the IDA (2007), approximately 13–14% of the nation's school children have a disability that meets special education eligibility criteria, with about half of these students being classified as having a learning disability, and a majority (85%) of these "LD" students having a primary disability in reading and language processing. However, the IDA goes on to suggest that 15–20% of the general population may manifest some symptoms of dyslexia (e.g., inaccurate reading, poor spelling). While not all these individuals will qualify for special education, they will likely struggle with many aspects of academic learning and will typically "benefit from systematic, explicit, instruction in reading, writing, and language" (p. 3). It has been suggested that up to 20% of people in the US show evidence of language-based disorders, generally those most linked to dyslexia (National Institutes of Child Health & Development, 2007). These rates of prevalence are much higher than what is indicated by the results of intervention studies targeting at-risk readers in the early years of school. However, it is important to note that few of the intervention studies have researched long-term outcomes for children beyond the time frame of the intervention.

Prevalence in Special Education

Given the estimate that it is likely that 80–90% of students identified as having a learning disability have reading disabilities (Kavale & Reese, 1992; Lyon, 1995) and using a figure of 85% of SLD students having a reading disability, it is estimated that around 4% of the total school population aged 6–17 years receive special education services due to a reading disability. Figure 3.1 shows estimates of the

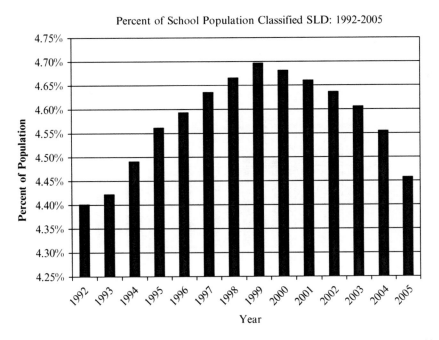

Fig. 3.1 The percentage of the total student population who fell in the SLD category from 1992 to 2005 (U.S. Department of Education, 2007)

percentage of total students who fell in this category from 1991 to 2005 (U.S. Department of Education, 2007). These rates have changed little over the last 15 years. Considering this figure in relation to the information presented here (NAEP results indicating that 33% of fourth-grade students are not at a basic level, while IDA and NICHD estimate that 15–20% of the population exhibit reading disabilities), it appears likely that many more children are not performing at an adequate level in reading than are being served in special education.

Figure 3.2 shows the number of students served under the SLD category according to age group from 1996 to 2006. As can be seen most of the students are aged 12–17 years. Within this age group, 56% of the students receiving special education services do so under the category of SLD, whereas for 6- to 11-year-old students, SLD represents only 33% of the total special education population. Perhaps this is a result of the discrepancy model that has been used to place students in special education under SLD. Under this model, it was unlikely that students would be performing so poorly in an academic area as to show the significant discrepancy required for eligibility until they had reached third grade.

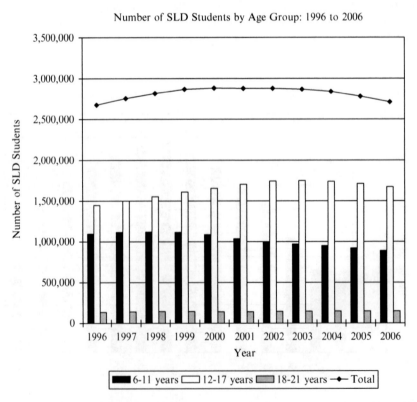

Fig. 3.2 The number of students served under the SLD category by age group from 1996 to 2006 (U.S. Department of Education, 2007)

Problems in Estimating Prevalence

Miles (2004) discusses three issues in determining the prevalence of dyslexia. First, when estimating prevalence across languages, it is possible that dyslexia manifests itself differently in different languages. Second, full assessment to determine prevalence would be far too costly to reasonably undertake it. Third, dyslexia symptoms can vary from moderate to severe. Such problems with determining prevalence are also addressed by Shaywitz (2003) in her discussion of a longitudinal study of school children in Connecticut. The findings from this study indicated that reading disability affected approximately one in five children. The researchers explored differences between how children are identified as having reading disabilities in the schools vs. in the research studies. All students participating in the Connecticut study were administered individual tests of intelligence and reading. Using these data, the researchers found that approximately 20% of the children were reading below what would be expected for their age, grade, or level of ability. Upon investigation of school histories of those children identified (using study-determined criteria) as performing below expected levels in reading, it was found that less than one-third of them had received any kind of reading support services. From findings such as these, it appears that the prevalence of dyslexia is higher than the 5% of students served in special education for reading disabilities. As previously noted, IDA (2007) suggests that 20% or more of students will need systematic, direct instruction in basic reading skills to be successful readers. Though unidentified children may not have shown deficits severe enough to warrant special education, it may be that these children would have benefited from early intervention.

Prevalence and Gender

Far more boys than girls are identified by schools as having reading disabilities. Within the category of specific learning disability, 67% of the 6- to 12-year-old students and 66% of the 13- to 17-year-old students so identified are boys (U.S. Department of Education, 2007). Thus, there is a roughly 2:1 ratio of boys to girls in the identification of specific learning disability: a population in which 80–90% of the students have reading disability. However, some researchers believe the higher incidence of identification among boys is an artifact of the school referral process. Shaywitz, Escobar, Shaywitz, Fletcher, and Makuch (1992) cite data from their Connecticut longitudinal study to demonstrate that when students are identified through research team assessments the rates of dyslexia among boys and girls are not different. Shaywitz and colleagues suggest that the higher rates of identification for boys within school-based populations are due to behavioral issues, not the presence of reading problems. Lubs et al. (1993) came to a similar conclusion in their study of families of students identified as having dyslexia. DeFries, Olson, Pennington, and Smith (1991) also found the ratio of boys and girls with dyslexia

to be similar in their work with the Colorado Reading Project. Likewise, Flynn and
Rahbar (1994) found nonsignificant differences in the prevalence of reading disability between boys and girls when objective criteria were used to ascertain the
presence of the disorder.

In their review of the literature on gender ratio in reading disability, Liederman,
Kantrowitz, and Flannery (2005) sought to "use methods designed to eliminate
or minimize ascertainment bias" (p. 110) in their selection of studies for review.
Liederman and colleagues questioned the results of the aforementioned studies
citing issues with lack of clearly defined diagnostic criteria, small sample size, and
complications of sampling in families with a history of dyslexia. Through a literature search back to 1963, the authors identified all studies that dealt with reading
disabilities using a variety of keywords. Using selection criteria to assure lack of
bias, clearly defined diagnostic criteria, and separate samples, the authors found 11
studies that met their criteria and were reviewed. Eight of these studies reported
gender bias toward males. Liederman and colleagues conclude that "gender sex
ratio is most accurately represented by the studies that found gender ratios between
1.74 and 2.00" (p. 116). Further findings from their review include an increase
in gender ratio as severity of reading disability increases and as IQ increases.
In reviewing longitudinal studies of children in New Zealand and England, Rutter
et al. (2004) found the rates of reading disability to be significantly higher in boys
with a 1.4 to 2.7:1 ratio in favor of boys over girls.

As school practitioners, it is important to be aware of the referral bias that may
occur in classrooms such that boys with reading problems are more likely to be
referred than are girls. It is still unclear from the research whether there is a higher
prevalence among boys, but current findings suggest that even if the prevalence is
higher among boys it is not as high as we see in school-referred populations. Therefore,
practitioners must have objective criteria for measuring reading progress and must be
aware of the behaviors that may make it more likely for a boy to be referred (e.g.,
externalizing behaviors) and less likely for a girl to be referred (e.g., internalizing
behaviors) even though the girl may be struggling with reading to the same degree.
Thus, it would appear to be important to increase search and serve efforts with girls.

Ethnicity

Across ethnic groups, the percentage of the total population of students served as
having a SLD ranges from 1.71% of Asian/Pacific Islander students to 7.41% of
American Indian/Alaska Native students (U.S. Department of Education, 2007).
Figure 3.3 shows the total percentage of students in each ethnic group served
under *IDEIA* and the percentage served under the category of SLD. Because of
questions regarding the criteria used to refer and qualify students for special education purposes, the overrepresentation of minority students in special education,
and issues surrounding the identification of dyslexia in English Learners, these data
should be interpreted with caution in addressing prevalence across ethnicities.

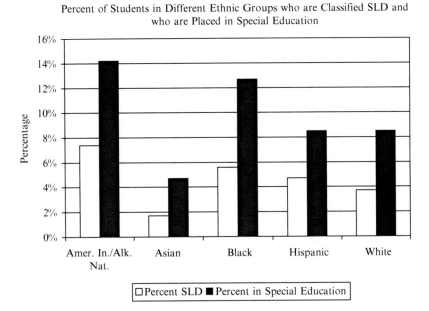

Fig. 3.3 Percentage of students in different ethnic groups who are provided special education services and the percentage served under the category of SLD

Cross Linguistically

Cross-linguistic studies in reading allow researchers to investigate reading development and dyslexia in languages that (a) are logographic (e.g., Chinese), (b) have a transparent alphabetic orthography (e.g., Italian), or (c) have an opaque alphabetic orthography (e.g., English). Perhaps one of the most interesting findings from this cross-linguistic research is the similarity in cognitive profiles of students who have reading problems in a variety of languages. Both phonological and naming speed deficits (though at different levels) are present across languages (Caravolas, 2005; Hanley, 2005). However, there are differences in how quickly children learn to decode and read in their native language (Goswami, 2005; Ziegler & Goswami, 2005). Children who are taught in transparent orthographies, within which there is a high level of consistency in both decoding print to speech (i.e., reading) and encoding speech to print (i.e., spelling), learn to read real and nonsense words much faster than children in a language such as English, which has a low level of consistency in both decoding and encoding (Zeigler & Goswami). However, despite the differing levels of ease with which children who are progressing at an average rate pick up the system for translating their written language into spoken language, the prevalence of dyslexia appears to be the same across languages when considering children learning to read in their native language (Ganshow & Miles, 2000).

Co-occurring Conditions

It is important to understand issues of co-occurring conditions when considering students with dyslexia as these conditions can significantly complicate symptom presentation and treatment outcomes. Common comorbid conditions include AD/HD, psychological disturbances, speech and language impairments, and other academic disorders. Johnson (2005) reports comorbidity for psychological disorders as being as high as 79% of children with learning disabilities. Thus, it is critical that practitioners have a good understanding of the conditions that are more likely to be present in children with dyslexia and understand the relationship between these comorbid conditions.

Attention-Deficit/Hyperactivity Disorder

One of the conditions most commonly associated with dyslexia is AD/HD. However, the relationship is complex. For example, though 36% of students diagnosed with AD/HD are likely to also have dyslexia, only 18% of those diagnosed with dyslexia are likely to have AD/HD (Shaywitz, Fletcher, & Shaywitz, 1994). One of the highest rates of comorbidity was found in a clinic-referred sample in which high rates of comorbidity (95% of the sample displayed more than one of the disorders) were found between AD/HD, attention deficit disorder, obsessive compulsive disorder, Tourette's Syndrome, and dyslexia (Pauc, 2005). Pauc suggests that such a high rate raises the question as to whether these are different disorders or manifestations of a more general developmental delay. Willcutt and Pennington (2000a, 2000b) also investigated the relationships among externalizing disorders, AD/HD, and reading disorder. They found that externalizing disorders were no more evident in the students with reading disorders than in those without reading disorder when controlling for the presence of AD/HD.

Willcutt and Pennington (2002b) note that these findings are in agreement with previous findings that the presence of externalizing disorders (such as conduct disorder and oppositional defiant disorder) among children and adolescents with reading disorders is "mediated by the presence of ADHD, whether the sample is initially selected for reading disability or one of the DBDs" (p. 1046). However, the authors found high rates of internalizing disorders in children diagnosed with dyslexia independent of the presence of AD/HD. Willcut and Pennington noted that the link between reading disorder and internalizing disorders was primarily associated with girls. In contrast, the link between reading disorder and externalizing disorders was stronger among boys. Pennington and Olson (2005) reported that 18% of girls with reading disability have comorbid AD/HD, whereas 40% of boys with reading disability have comorbid AD/HD. Penntington and Olson also found a common genetic risk factor among children with AD/HD and dyslexia and evidence of higher rates of AD/HD in preschool children later diagnosed with dyslexia.

Cutting and Denckla (2003) discuss the common deficits in executive function that can occur in both learning disabilities and AD/HD as a possible explanation of the high co-occurrence of these two disorders. Though deficits in executive function are most commonly associated with problems in higher-order academic skills such as reading comprehension, Cutting and Denckla suggest that they can also impact basic reading development. Thus, it may be that a portion of the population has an underlying executive function problem that leads to the presence of both reading disability and AD/HD. Another factor that could link these two conditions is that the presence of AD/HD could impact a student's availability for instruction during critical early instructional periods. Likewise, it is possible that children who struggle in learning to read may exhibit AD/HD-like behaviors that are a result of their academic distress. In these two cases, the presence of both disorders in an individual student is not linked to an underlying cause, but rather the result of one disorder leading to symptoms of the other. This possibility speaks to the need for practitioners to engage in differential diagnosis when presented with students exhibiting symptoms of multiple disorders.

Fletcher et al. (2007) report on the results of a series of studies at the Yale Center for Learning and Attention Disorders, which examined the relationship between reading and attention disorders. The cognitive pattern of strengths and weaknesses was the same for children with combined reading and attention disorders as the pattern for those with reading disorder alone. The most consistent area of weakness was phonological awareness. Conversely, children with only attention disorders displayed a profile similar to nonimpaired subjects. Differences in naming speed have also been found between children with either reading disability or attention disorders (Denckla & Rudel, 1976a, 1976b; Felton, Wood, Brown, Campbell, & Harter, 1987); however, in a more recent study number naming speed deficits were found to exist among a sample of AD/HD children, even without a coexisting reading disability (Brock & Christo, 2003).

Given that AD/HD and dyslexia have a high likelihood of co-occurrence (particularly among boys), it will be important for school professionals to have the skills and knowledge that enable them to differentiate between these disorders in their evaluations. In addition, it is important to be cognizant of the fact that the stronger co-occurrence of reading disorder and externalizing disorders among boys may lead to increased rates of referral for boys due to their classroom behavior.

Dyscalculia

Fletcher (2005) reported findings comparing the cognitive profiles of students with no academic disorders, reading disorder only, math disorder only, and combined math and reading disorder. He found that though the profile of cognitive strengths and weaknesses was similar for groups with reading disorder and with reading and math disorder the students with math disorder were generally lower on full-scale IQ and all cognitive processes measured. In addition, the profiles of students with math disorder vs. that of students with math and reading disorders were different. Students with both math and reading disorders displayed deficits in phonological processing, whereas those with math disorders only did not show this deficit.

Specific Language Impairment

Dyslexia is conceptualized as a language-based disorder, and the presence of specific language impairment among students classified as having a reading disability has been reported to be as high as 55% in a school population (IDA, 2007; McArthur, Hogben, Edwards, Health, & Mengler, 2000). Studies exploring predictors of reading difficulty have found that children with early reading problems display deficits in various aspects of oral language prior to school entry (Muter & Snowling, 1998; Scarborough, 1991, 1998a, 1998b).

In considering the relationship between dyslexia and language impairments, Snowling (2006) distinguishes between speech skills and language skills. Snowling notes:

> "...learning to read in an alphabetic system, such as English, requires the development of mappings between speech sounds, and letters – the so-called alphabetic principle – and this depends on speech skills. Wider language skills are required to understand the meanings of words and sentences..." (pp. 1–2)

Therefore, it is the speech-related skill of phonological processing that is linked to reading disorder, while deficits in language skills related to semantics and syntax are linked to difficulties in reading comprehension. Snowling (2006) proposes a conceptualization of dyslexia and specific language impairment in which language skills and the speech skill of phonological awareness interact to produce a continuum across the two disorders. Children with only phonological impairment will have dyslexia and those with only specific language impairment will have reading comprehension difficulties. However, within this model, strong language skills can compensate for weak phonological processing. Scarborough (2005) puts forth a similar hypothesis in proposing a model of reading difficulty that considers the interaction of multiple factors (including language impairment) in the development and trajectory of reading problems.

Catts, Adolf, Hogan, and Weismer (2005) also explored the relationship between specific language impairment and dyslexia by proposing and testing three models explaining this relationship. The results of their studies suggested that the two disorders were separate but comorbid. Though there was overlap between the presence of dyslexia and specific language impairment, beyond what would be expected from base rates (see also Bishop & Snowling, 2004), it was not sufficient enough to suggest the presence of a common cause. In addition, phonological deficits were strongly associated with dyslexia, but not with specific language impairment.

The work of Pennington and colleagues in the Colorado Twin Studies (Pennington & Olson, 2005; Tunick & Pennington, 2002) appears to further support Snowling's conceptualization differentiating between types of speech and language disorders and their impact on reading development. Recent molecular studies seeking to find common genetic risk factors have found a common factor for speech and reading disorders, but not for language-based semantic/syntactic problems and reading disorder. Distinguishing between these disorders and the contributions of each to the identification of risk factors and instructional planning are discussed in Chaps. 5 and 6. In addition, it is important to consider the interaction between speech skills (e.g., phonological processing) and language skills (e.g., semantics and syntax) on the development of proficient or impaired reading skills.

Concluding Comments

Dyslexia is a common learning disability. Although only around 5% of children have severe challenges associated with this condition (e.g., challenges that warrant special education placement), as many as 20% of the school age population appear to display some symptoms of dyslexia. Further complicating the presentation of this disorder is the fact that children with dyslexia are more likely than the general population to have characteristics of other conditions such as AD/HD, other psychological disorders, and speech impairment. For children who present with more than one condition, it will be important to consider their impacts on the child both separately and in concert. Comorbid conditions can exacerbate the consequences of dyslexia. Thus, treatment plans must address all conditions as appropriate. This will be critical in both helping others to understand the child's functioning and in intervention planning.

Chapter 4
Case Finding and Screening

Given the deleterious consequences of poor reading on students' educational opportunities, the importance of identifying these children early is obvious. In addition, it is clear that intervention can improve reading outcomes for those at risk for dyslexia. It is also important that identification and intervention occur early. Delays in providing intervention in reading have negative impacts on multiple areas related to reading development including vocabulary (Cunningham & Stanovich, 1999), fluency (Torgesen, Rashotte, & Alexander, 2001), and comprehension (Gough & Tunmer, 1986). In addition, as was noted in Chap. 1, the odds are poor that the student, who by fourth grade is still reading below grade level, will ever be able to attain grade-level reading achievement.

Two types of activities are part of child find efforts to identify children at risk for dyslexia. First, it is important to educate caregivers about what characteristics indicate risk. These activities include fact sheets for parents or teachers, and might be referred to as case finding. Second, more formal efforts should be instituted at key points in a child's life, and this might be referred to as screening.

It is often with the start of formal reading instruction, during the early primary years, that children are first identified as being at risk for dyslexia. However, it is possible to suggest which children may be at risk for dyslexia prior to school entry, and likewise it is important to recognize students with dyslexia who may have traversed the school system without previously being identified. Therefore, in this chapter, we will discuss identification of those who may be at risk for the disorder and require further assessment at both preschool and school-aged levels.

Issues in Case Finding and Screening

Because learning to read is a complex process, the factors that place a child at risk for reading difficulties are not straightforward. Rather factors that may put one child at risk for dyslexia may be mitigated in another child by resiliency factors existing within and/or outside the child. Risk is a phenomenon that is perhaps best conceptualized as multifactorial as opposed to unidimensional. That said there is good information about specific characteristics, both external and internal, that can

C. Christo et al., *Identifying, Assessing, and Treating Dyslexia at School,*
DOI: 10.1007/978-0-387-88600-8_4, © Springer Science+Business Media, LLC 2009

increase a child's risk of dyslexia. Perhaps the most appropriate risk model is one
in which the factors that put children at risk are weighed against factors that may
reduce risk to arrive at a result more closely approximating each child's likelihood
of developing dyslexia given any specific risk factor. Even within a domain such as
language skills, children may exhibit patterns of strengths and weaknesses across
domain subskills. Snowling, Gallagher, and Frith (2003) demonstrated that among
children at risk for dyslexia those whose language profiles showed strengths in
nonphonological aspects of oral language despite deficits in phonological aspects
fared better than those with equivalent phonological deficits coupled with deficits
in other aspects of oral language as well.

   Another issue in case finding and screening is, what will be done once a child
is identified? Case finding without provisions for more comprehensive diagnostic
and psychoeducational evaluations, and comprehensive intervention services is
futile. The appropriate service to be provided will vary as a function of the level
of risk, history of interventions, age of the child, and stage of reading development.
Therefore, before any case-finding activities are undertaken, school professionals
should have a system in place for further evaluating and providing services to
identified individuals.

   One issue related to service provision is expense. Cost of service is more than
just financial. Cost of service can also involve the invasiveness or unpleasantness
of the treatment. In the case of learning problems, it may involve the cost of being
labeled should special education services be necessary. In most cases, the nonfinancial cost of being identified as at risk for reading disabilities is fairly innocuous.
Generally, the treatment will consist of some form of enrichment geared toward
improved learning whether it be enriching vocabulary or improving decoding
skill. However, these nonfinancial costs merit consideration. For example, will identifying preschoolers as at risk for reading disability cause parents to increase their
reading and word play with the children or will it create a high level of anxiety
that hinders positive parent child interaction? For early primary students, will
identification mean they get the support they need to make reading enjoyable or
will it mean that they get labeled as "dumb" for needing extra help? Finally, the
financial costs cannot be ignored. In education, at all levels from early childhood
to post secondary, financial resources are scarce and intervention services are
expensive. Therefore, it is important that we have methods for identification of
students at risk that come as close as possible to identifying students with true
risk whose needs merit the costs of the service.

   A useful way to conceptualize the issue of successful screening is to consider
how accurate a measure is at identifying both those at risk and those not at risk.
As outlined in Table 4.1, children screened for being at risk for dyslexia can fall
into one of four categories:

- *True positives* are those children who are in fact at risk for dyslexia and are
  identified as being at risk by the screening.
- *False positives* are those children who are not truly at risk for dyslexia, but are
  identified as being at risk by the screening.

Table 4.1 Screening outcomes

		Reality	
		Has dyslexia	Does not have dyslexia
Screening result	Identified with dyslexia	True positives	False positives
	Not identified with dyslexia	False negatives	True negatives

- *True negatives* are those children who are in fact not at risk for dyslexia and are not identified as being at risk by the screening.
- *False negatives* are those children who are truly at risk for dyslexia, but are not identified as being at risk by the screening.

The goal of case finding and subsequent screening is to maximize the true positives and true negatives, and to minimize the false positives and false negatives.

Ratios representing the degree of sensitivity and specificity of one's screening procedures can be computed. The measure of sensitivity is derived by dividing the number of *true positives* by the number of *true positives* and *false negatives* and is an index of how good the test is at identifying those individuals who have the disorder. The specificity index is derived by dividing the number of *true negatives* by the number of *true negatives* and *false positives* and is an index of how good the test is at identifying those individuals who do not have the disorder (see Table 4.2).

Table 4.2 Measures of sensitivity and specificity

Sensitivity=	$\dfrac{\text{True positives}}{\text{True positives} + \text{False negatives}}$	Accuracy in identifying those who *have* disorder
Specificity=	$\dfrac{\text{True negatives}}{\text{True negatives} + \text{False positives}}$	Accuracy in identifying those who *do not have* disorder

Gredler (2000) recommends that these indices should be at least 0.75 for screening of young children. Sensitivity and specificity are important in screening as there may be a relatively high correlation between two variables (phonological awareness and word reading for example), but relatively low sensitivity and specificity when using the factor for screening. For example, Hammill, Mather, Allen, and Roberts (2002) reported a correlation of 0.65 for phonology and word identification. However, the sensitivity index was only 0.66, which falls below the recommended index of 0.75 or higher. This means that a relatively large number of children may not show problems with phonology in screening, but will develop reading problems. Helping schools understand the importance of attempting to maximize the hit rate or confirming screening results with further evaluation is an important role for school psychologists and other professionals working with systems to develop screening programs. It also may be that over-referral, or identifying children as at risk who are not (false positives) is of less concern than not identifying children who are (false negatives). In such a case, a school may be willing to tolerate a lower specificity index for a higher sensitivity index.

Generally, child find focuses on active screening of wide populations to identify those children at risk for a disability and to provide interventions targeted at remediating or reducing any negative sequelae that are likely to follow if the child is left untreated. In considering issues of identifying children at risk of reading problems in a broader sense, one can also consider how to differentiate between children with greater or lesser risk of reading disability and intervene accordingly. These issues are discussed more thoroughly in Chap. 6, psychoeducational evaluation, as they factor into decision making in intervention-focused assessments. This chapter addresses (a) early markers that may put children at risk for dyslexia prior to school entry and (b) characteristics present at school entry as children become involved in formal schooling. Discussion will include how to alert parents, physicians, and other community members who may be in contact with young children to signals of possible risk status as well as formal screening measures.

Identifying Children Prior to School Entry

Attempts to investigate very early manifestations of future reading disability have identified characteristics such as early delays in language milestones and differences in infant brain waves in response to speech sounds among those children who later manifested reading problems (McCardle, Scarborough, & Catts, 2001). Such findings, though sparse, suggest that it is important for parents, pediatricians, and other caregivers to be alert to behaviors that suggest the possibility of risk for future reading problems. In the following section, we review some of the early factors that serve as markers for children at risk of reading disabilities during the early childhood years. These factors include family history, language development, and otitis media; are summarized in Table 4.3; and are described as follows.

Family History

Having a parent with dyslexia is a significant risk factor for the development of later reading problems. The largest studies to investigate familial and genetic linkage in dyslexia are being conducted in the Colorado Learning Disabilities Resource Center (DeFries, Alarcon, & Olson, 1997). These ongoing studies have used twins (both with and without dyslexia) and their families to study the heritability of dyslexia through both behavioral and molecular methods. For readers wishing to learn more about the results of these studies, they are referred to the website, http://ibgwww.colorado.edu/twinsites.html.

These studies have enabled the researchers to differentiate heritable versus environmental influences on risk of dyslexia. Evidence for the heritability of reading difficulties, as measured by reading and spelling achievement tests, is strong. Wadsworth, Olson, Pennington, and DeFries (2000) estimate that over 50% of the

Table 4.3 Early childhood dyslexia risk factors

Factor	Description
Family history of dyslexia	Dyslexia runs in families, and having one or more biological parent(s) and/or a sibling with dyslexia predicts reading delays. As many as 66% of children with a parent who has dyslexia will also have reading difficulties
Global language deficits	There is good evidence that delays in multiple speech and language areas generate a high risk for later reading problems
Specific language deficits	These factors will have differential and interactive effects on later reading development. Isolated deficits are not as powerful predictors of later reading skill as are global language delays
Oral language deficits	Durable speech production/articulation problems may predict phonological awareness problems
Vocabulary deficits	Number of words in preschool spoken vocabulary is associated with later reading proficiency
Phonological processing delays	Rhyme detection and production, word segmenting, and sound recognition and categorization predict later reading success
Letter knowledge deficits	Delays in learning the alphabet predict later reading deficits
Otitis media	Chronic middle ear infections between 6 and 18 months of age may be associated with phonological, semantic, and reading skill delays. However, the research in this area is not consistent

difference in achievement scores on these measures was due to heritable genetic influences. In a longitudinal study conducted in England by Snowling et al. (2003), 66% of those students identified as at risk at age 4 years due to having a parent with dyslexia were found to be significantly delayed in reading at 8 years of age. Puolakanaho et al. (2007) found that adding family risk status (as determined by having a family member with dyslexia) to a battery including measures of letter knowledge, phonological awareness, and rapid naming led to a considerable increase in predictive power of measures at 3.5 years of age. In addition to evidence of heredity in reading performance, data also support hereditability of underlying abilities of phonological processing and rapid naming (Davis et al., 2001; Gayan & Olson, 2005).

Genetic studies have identified possible candidate genes for being linked with dyslexia (Pennington & Olson, 2005). Of course, as mentioned in Chap. 2, it is important to remember that there is no "reading gene" per se as reading is a very recent development in terms of human evolution. In considering the evidence from the Colorado Twin Studies as well as from the Twins Early Development Study in the United Kingdom, it is evident that family history of dyslexia is a strong risk factor that should be considered in any screening for children at risk of dyslexia. However, it is also important to bear in mind the caveat addressed by

Pennington and Olson regarding the nature of their population. The sample of twins in the Colorado study was overwhelmingly from suburban schools with average to above average academic ratings. There are very few participants from low SES schools. Thus "the substantial genetic influences reported...should not be generalized to samples with different degrees of variation in education or socioeconomic level, and we should not conclude that relatively poor reading performance in areas of poverty and poor education has any relation to genetic factors" (p. 465).

Language Development

When considering the risk factors of developing dyslexia related to language development, it is worthwhile to revisit the distinction discussed in Chap. 3 between "speech skills" and "language skills" (Snowling, 2005). Speech skills are those involved in the production of speech, and tend to relate to phonological processing and development of the alphabetic principle, while language skills represent those abilities important to understanding the meaning of language such as semantics and syntax. Snowling suggests that in considering the impact of language deficits on reading development it is important to consider that the full range of language skills, in either speech or language, will have differential and interactive effects. Children who have deficits in only one area of language may compensate for their deficits and become successful readers. Thus, "language skills outside of the phonological module can modify the manifestation of familial dyslexia" (Snowling, p. 69).

Scarborough (2005) cautions that in predicting reading ability from the language performance of preschool children it is important to be aware that "different language skills predict future reading from different preschool ages" (p. 8). For example, she reports that children who later developed reading disabilities were differentiated from the normally achieving group as follows: "syntactic and speech production (but not vocabulary) at the youngest ages (2.5 and 3 years), syntactic and vocabulary skills (but not speech) over the succeeding years (ages 3.5–4 years) and vocabulary and phonological awareness (but not syntax) at age 5" (p. 8). The following section considers these different aspects of language development and their unique predictive ability for identifying children who are at risk for dyslexia. For children who have global language deficits, the likelihood of reading problems is high (Badian, 1994; Catts, Fey, Zhang, & Tomblin, 2001; Catts & Hogan, 2003).

Oral Language

In line with Scarborough's findings, other studies evaluating the presence of reading problems in children evidencing speech production problems as preschoolers have provided mixed results. Some studies suggest that expressive speech difficulties are predictive of phonological awareness problems (Bird, Bishop, & Freeman, 1995), while other studies demonstrate that problems with speech production are not related to later reading difficulties (Bishop & Snowling, 2004; Catts, 1993).

Recent research suggests that the critical factor in whether early speech production difficulties are predictive of reading problems is whether these problems are resolved early during reading instruction. Specifically, Nathan, Stackhouse, Goulandris, and Snowling (2004) evaluated the reading skills at age 7 years of a group of children who had been diagnosed with articulation problems between 4 and 5 years of age. They found that for those children whose speech problems had been resolved there were no deficits in reading skills; however, those children who had lingering speech problems performed less well on reading tasks at age 7 than did the control group. In addition, the children who had deficits only in speech production did better than those who also had more global language delays (Stackhouse, 2006). Scarborough (2005) suggests that problems in phonological processing alone cannot account for research findings indicating that children with nonphonological language impairments have just as much risk for reading failure as those with phonological impairments and that such language measures are as good at predicting later reading outcomes as are phonological measures.

Vocabulary

Children's vocabulary prior to first grade is predictive of early reading development as well as later reading proficiency (Dickinson & Tabors, 2001; Scarborough, 2005; Snowling et al., 2003). Certainly, having a word in one's spoken vocabulary will facilitate its recognition when reading. It has also been suggested that a richer vocabulary may create richer phonological representations, thus positively impacting phonological processing (Goswami, 2000, 2001; Walley, 1993). It may also be that measures of vocabulary tap an underlying facility with language that proves facilitative in developing those skills more directly associated with early reading such as phonological processing.

Phonological Processing

There is extensive evidence that problems in phonological processing when children are beginning to learn to read put them at risk for dyslexia (Castles & Coltheart, 2004; Fletcher & Shaywitz, 1994; Shatil & Share, 2003; Wagner et al., 1997), and there is a correlation between preschool performance on such tasks and later reading ability (Bradley & Bryant, 1983; Muter & Snowling, 1998). In addition, it is possible to differentiate between children's phonological processing skills during the preschool years. Tasks that are used to measure phonological processing in young children include rhyme detection and production, segmenting, phoneme recognition, and sound categorization (Badian, 1994; Muter, 2000; Torgesen & Wagner, 1994).

Results suggest that children who have good phonological skills during the preschool years will become good readers. However, the link between poor phonological skills during the preschool years and later reading difficulties is not nearly as strong. That is, many preschool children who have poor phonological skills and may be identified as at risk for dyslexia will go on to develop into adequate readers (the specificity index). In addition, studies demonstrating the link between phonological awareness in preschool and later reading have used many different tasks to measure the skill in preschool children, which makes it difficult to identify the particular phonological processing skills that are the strongest indicators of risk status. However, data suggest that promoting phonological processing in young children and paying attention to those who seem not to respond at the same level as their peers can be beneficial to later reading development (Badian, 1994; Byrne & Fielding-Barnsley, 1993; Christensen, 2000).

Complicating the picture are results suggesting that the risk of reading difficulties due to lags in the development of phonologically based language skills during the early years may fall along a continuum as opposed to a fixed point, providing support for Snowling's (2005) model described above. For example, Pennington and Lefly (2001) found that children in a high risk group (as defined by having a parent with dyslexia) who later became reading disabled had deficits in speech perception, verbal short-term memory, rapid naming, and phonological awareness prior to school entry. The children who were considered high risk of reading disability, but developed average level reading skills were lower than controls on these same measures, but not as low as those who became disabled readers.

In addition, Scarborough and Parker (2003) found that children who were at familial risk for dyslexia, yet developed average reading comprehension skills, had better nonphonological language skills (vocabulary and narrative skills) as preschoolers than those who did not develop average reading skills. However, the unimpaired high risk group did not perform differently than the impaired group on tasks of decoding and spelling during the early years of reading. These data suggest that the children who presented a more mixed language profile (low in some phonological processes, but average or above in syntactic and semantic measures) were able to compensate for phonological weaknesses, whereas those children with low overall language skills were not.

Though there has been limited research on English Learners, studies suggest that the phonological processing skills learned in one language will carry over into a new language (Gottardo, 2002). This is particularly true if there are similar sounds within the two languages (Bialystok, 2002). Thus, it may be useful to assess phonological development in a child's first language to identify any children who may be at risk for phonologically based problems in learning English.

Letter Knowledge

Not surprisingly one of the best preschool predictors of future reading success is letter knowledge (Byrne, Fielding-Barnsley, Ashley, & Larsen, 1997; Muter, 2000; Snowling et al., 2003). Letter knowledge may be facilitative of learning to read (Ehri, 1992) and may also be a task that serves to represent the outward manifestation of other cognitive processes (verbal memory), predispositions (interest in books), and environmental (access to print) factors important to reading.

Otitis Media

There have been conflicting results in studies examining the relationship between otitis media (inflammation of the middle ear) and later academic outcomes (Roberts, Burchinal, & Zeisel, 2002; Winskel, 2006). In their study, Roberts and colleagues did not find any long-term detrimental effects of a history of otitis media on word recognition in the early elementary school years. However, they note that their results "should be interpreted with caution when generalizing to other populations because the children began attending child care in infancy, had OME [otitis media with effusion] in early childhood, and were primarily from low-income families" (p. 706, brackets added). In contrast to the findings of the Robert and colleagues' study, Winskel reports that children in grades 1 and 2 with a history of otitis media were deficient on phonological, semantic, and reading abilities. The impact of otitis media seems most pronounced when it occurs between 6 and 18 months of age. It is suggested that the fluctuating hearing loss that accompanies otitis media (and not otitis media per se) prevents the child from developing well-defined representations of speech sounds and thus makes mapping print to speech more challenging for the developing child.

Preschool Screening Batteries

Badian (2000) has investigated the most useful measures for a preschool screening battery. In regard to phonological awareness as a predictor of reading ability, Badian notes inconsistent results in the use of such measures. One problem is that preschool children are too young to engage in tasks at the phoneme level (which in older children are the most predictive), and the rhyming tasks that are acceptable to use with young children tend to lack long-term validity as predictors of reading.

In an effort to improve the predictive value of a preschool test battery, Badian (2000) included a measure of orthographic processing. The final preschool battery included measures of socioeconomic status, language, verbal IQ, sentence memory, serial-naming speed, phonological awareness (syllable counting), orthographic processing, and untimed naming of letters and colors. The participants were followed up at first, second, and seventh grades. The three preschool measures that "most consistently accounted for significant variance after verbal IQ and demographic measures were entered, were letter naming, sentence memory, and the orthographic test" (p. 46). The phonological measure of syllable counting correlated with reading at each grade, but any predictive power it had was overshadowed by letter naming and sentence memory. Object-naming speed also correlated with various literacy measures across grade levels, but did not provide any unique predictive power beyond letter naming and sentence memory. Thus, Badian concluded that the most useful preschool measures for predicting reading at each of the grade levels assessed are letter naming and sentence memory. However, it is important to note that even with this extensive battery, many more children were identified as at risk for reading problems than actually ended up with reading disabilities.

Phonological Abilities Test (Muter, Hulme, & Snowling, 1997)

The phonological abilities test (PAT) is an example of a battery designed to assess specific areas related to reading development; phonological awareness, speech skills, and letter knowledge; and has four phonological awareness tasks (Rhyme Detection, Rhyme Production, Word Completion, and Beginning and Ending Phonemes), a speech rate task, and a test of Letter Knowledge. This measure was standardized on 826 children aged 4 years to 7 years, 11 months, by University of York (United Kingdom) undergraduate and graduate students in their hometowns during their summer vacations. Internal consistency reliability estimates ranged from 0.67 for the speech rate task to 0.97 for the beginning sound phoneme deletion task. Three-week test–retest reliability estimates ranged from 0.58 for Word Completion to 0.86 for Letter Knowledge (Ward, 2003). This assessment takes approximately 30 min to administer and another 10 for scoring.

Estimates of construct validity were obtained via examination of subtest score intercorrelations and ranged from 0.3 to 0.7. Concurrent and predictive validity were examined by correlating the PAT with the British Abilities Scales (BAS) test of Single Word Reading. From multiple regression analyses, it was found that with the exception of the Word Completion-Syllables and the Word Completion-Phonemes subtests all PAT measures were significant predictors of BAS results. However, it is important to note that Ward (2003) questions use of a single word reading measure to estimate test validity, as it may not be a good estimate of phonological skill, and suggests that "educational personnel would be ill-advised to use only…the *Phonological Abilities Test* to predict children who were at-risk for reading problems…" (p. 10).

Checklists

In addition to formal screening assessments, another approach is to identify behaviors that might be "warning signals" to those caring for young children. Reading Rockets, an organization devoted to early reading development, provides the warning signs listed in Table 4.4. In addition, the website provides parents with a checklist entitled "Get Ready to Read," which was developed by Grover J. Whitehurst for the National Center for Learning Disabilities and its Get Ready to Read! program. The screening tool is published by Pearson Early Learning, but is available free to parents online at http://www.readingrockets.org/families/recognizesigns/getready/

Table 4.4 Recognize early signs of trouble

For almost 40% of children, learning to read is a challenge. So in addition to talking, reading,
and writing with your child, families play another important role – being on the lookout
for early signs of possible trouble. Here are two of the biggest to watch out for:

Language or speech problems: Children who talk late, who say very few words, who have
trouble pronouncing words, or who have difficulty expressing feelings verbally may
have trouble learning to read

Hearing impairment: Children who have difficulty hearing the individual sounds in words may
have trouble understanding how those sounds connect with letters in written words

Kids who might have trouble learning to read also may show some of these early warning signs:

Difficulty in rhyming words

Difficulty in learning the alphabet, numbers, or days of the week

Difficulty in following multistep directions

Difficulty in telling or retelling a story

You can avoid years of frustration for you and your child by recognizing these problems early
and getting the right help

Adapted from http://www.readingrockets.org/families/recognizesigns

directions. It consists of 20 questions measuring concepts of print as well as letter
name and sound knowledge and phonological awareness. It is described as follows
on the Web site:

> "Because skills with sounds, language, and letters are so important, we encourage you to
> take a few minutes to use this tool to screen the four-year-olds you care about – children,
> grandchildren, nieces, nephews, or students. We recommend that you screen each child
> twice, first in the fall (a year before entering kindergarten) and then again before kinder-
> garten starts. (http://www.readingrockets.org/families/recognizesigns/getready, p. 2)

Figure 4.1 provides a sample item from this screening tool.

Shaywitz (2003) provides the following as clues to possible reading problems
that may be present during the preschool years:

- Trouble learning common nursery rhymes such as "Jack and Jill" and "Humpty
  Dumpty"
- A lack of appreciation of rhyme
- Mispronounced words; persistent baby talk
- Difficulty in learning (and remembering) names of letters
- Failure to know the letters in his own name (p. 122)

Both these checklists (Reading Rockets and Shaywitz) demonstrate the difficulties in clearly identifying early childhood precursors to dyslexia that are consistent
predictors. For example, in some studies, rhyme has been shown to predict later
reading skill and in others it has not. However, the purpose of such checklists is to
provide a broad net for catching children who potentially may have difficulty in
learning to read. The Reading Rockets checklist includes simple descriptors of
most of the language-related difficulties that children may exhibit. Thus, children
who show difficulties in all areas on this checklist may indeed be at risk as they may

Say to your child: "Let's look at some pictures. (Point to the pictures in the sample item.) I will ask you a question about them, and you put your finger on the picture that is the best answer to the question. Let's try one."

"These are pictures of a boy, fish, apple, car. Which one is the care? Find car"

Click the child's selection. Then click "next."

Fig. 4.1 Sample item from the "Get Ready to Read" checklist, developed by Grover J. Whitehurst for the National Center for Learning Disabilities and its Get Ready to Read! program. Copyright © 2001 NCS Pearson, Inc. All rights reserved. Published and distributed exclusively by NCS Pearson, Inc., Minneapolis, MN 55440. Reproduced with permission by NCS Pearson, Inc

have deficits in both speech-related language skills as well as semantic and syntactic skills (Snowling, 2005). These checklists can prove useful for instigating low levels of early intervention as well as encouraging caregivers to engage in the activities that will promote language development. Therefore, practitioners should strive to publicize these checklists within the child care community as well as with families and medical providers. Reading Rockets in cooperation with the National Association of School Psychologists (NASP) has developed a toolkit for school psychologists, which contains handouts that can be used with families to educate them on these important issues. In addition to the screening tool described, this toolkit is also available at the Reading Rockets website.

Kindergarten Screening

Attempts to investigate manifestations of reading disability upon school entry have been more successful than preschool screening in identifying students with dyslexia. The following sections provide a review of some of the factors that serve as markers for children at risk of reading disabilities during the early school years as well as specific screening strategies.

Visual Processing

Kindergarten screening inventories have included tasks of visual processing as indicators of developmental readiness. However, current research suggests that there is little evidence to support visual perceptual or visual memory problems as a marker for dyslexia (Fletcher, Foorman, Shaywitz, & Shaywitz, 1999; Vellutino, Scanlon, & Tanzman, 1994). Vellutino, Fletcher, Snowling, and Scanlon (2004) discuss the incidence of low-level visual deficits in individuals with dyslexia. Deficits in magnocellular pathways, which are important in motion detection, have been documented in dyslexic individuals. Eden and Zeffiro (1998) suggest that the visual and linguistic deficits that seem to be present in children with dyslexia may result from another underlying neural dysfunction common to both these systems. Vellutino et al. (1994) interpret the findings on visual deficits as follows:

> "But whereas the linguistic deficits have been demonstrated to be causally related to reading disability, the visual deficits have not been demonstrated to be causally related to reading disability, though they may serve as biological markers that aid differential diagnosis." (p. 10)

Assessments for deficits in the magnocellular pathway are performed under laboratory conditions. Therefore, though there is some evidence that children with dyslexia may also have specific visual processing deficits, there is no evidence of a causal link and the evidence is clear that there is no link between the kinds of visual processing that have been commonly assessed to suggest reading problems (visual memory and visual spatial processing) and reading disability. Thus, the authors conclude that *visual tasks are not a useful component in screening* for children at risk of reading disability.

Phonological Awareness

As noted previously, basic phonological skills have been identified as strong predictors of reading performance (Bradley & Bryant, 1983; Liberman, Shankweiler, & Liberman, 1989; Mann & Liberman, 1984; Stanovich, Cunningham, & Freeman, 1984; Wagner & Torgesen, 1987) when comparing poor readers with both age and reading-level matches. That is, poor readers are less proficient than their skilled reader age mates and also less proficient than younger readers of equal reading proficiency at tasks requiring phonological awareness. Various measures of phonological awareness are correlated with and predictive of early reading development (Badian, 1994; Felton & Brown, 1990; Muter, 1994; Nation & Hulme, 1997; O'Connor & Jenkins, 1999; Torgesen, Wagner, Rashotte, Burgess, & Hecht, 1997), and phonological awareness is linked to development and understanding of the alphabetic principle, a necessary first step in learning to read (Schatschneider & Torgesen, 2004). As noted previously for students who are English Learners, their proficiency with phonological processing in their first language is useful in predicting their risk status in learning English.

However, when attempting to identify measures of phonological awareness useful in screening young children for risk of dyslexia, the picture is less clear. Scarborough (1998a, 1998b) reviewed several studies investigating the predictive power of phonological awareness measured prior to or during the first year of schooling and its ability to predict reading difficulties. This meta-analysis looked at 27 different research samples from 24 studies. Her summary indicated that phonological awareness accounts for 18–21% of the variance in later reading scores. The predictive value of such measures differed across skill level. Children who did well on phonological measures at kindergarten entry tended to be successful readers; however, as with the preschool data it was not always the case that children who did poorly struggled with learning to read (poor specificity). Thus, the measures resulted in a number of false positives leading Scarborough to suggest that such measures are good predictors of who will *not* have trouble learning to read, but not so good at predicting who will have difficulty learning this skill.

Al Otaiba and Fuchs (2002) reviewed 23 studies that included children from preschool to third grade who were considered at risk for reading disability and received interventions. They found that in 70% of the studies examining the relationship of phonological awareness to responsiveness to the intervention, phonological awareness correlated significantly with nonresponsiveness to intervention. However, they did not report data on the accuracy of using performance on phonological awareness tasks to accurately identify those who developed average reading skills and those who did not (sensitivity and specificity). Nevertheless, the extensive correlational evidence showing a strong relationship between phonological awareness and early reading clearly supports the importance of fostering and monitoring the development of this skill in young children.

Vocabulary

Vocabulary measures are also useful indicators of reading risk at school entry (Torgesen, 2002a, 2002b). Al Otaiba and Fuchs (2006) found that vocabulary development was a powerful predictor of which children receiving classroom-based interventions would respond adequately to reading intervention.

Naming Speed Tasks

As discussed in Chap. 2, naming speed has been shown to correlate with reading difficulties (Ackerman, Dykman, & Gardner, 1990; Spring & Davis, 1988; Torgesen & Houck, 1980; Wolf, Bowers, & Biddle, 2000; Wolf & Obergon, 1992) and to be predictive of reading development (Allor, 2002; Felton, 1992; Manis, Seidenberg, & Doi, 1999; O'Connor & Jenkins, 1999; Torgesen et al., 1997). However, as with the data on phonological awareness, many children who show delayed naming speed have adequate reading skills (Waber, 2001). The naming speed tests most closely predictive of later reading when administered at kindergarten entry are those that involve symbol naming such as the naming of letters and numbers (Badian, 1994; Elbro, Borstrom, & Petersen, 1998; Felton). Badian reports on a study by Felton, which found that "when IQ and age were partialled out, kindergarten object naming speed correlated insignificantly with composite reading vocabulary/reading comprehension at grade 3 level in contrast to other naming tests" (p. 33). However, there is evidence that naming speed may be a better predictor when studying poor readers than when investigating the link with good readers.

Because knowing letter names is facilitative of reading development (Ehri, 2005), letter-naming speed may be more a marker of how well a child is acquiring foundational reading skills than of an underlying cognitive process. In addition, as children learn to read, the relationship between naming speed and basic word reading skills weakens (Kame'enui, Simmons, Good, & Harn, 2001; Manis & Freedman, 2001; Manis et al., 1999; Wagner et al., 1997). The Dynamic Indicators of Basic Early Literacy Skills (DIBELS) incorporate such measures into their battery. The DIBELS battery in its entirety will be discussed later. Both DIBELS and similar Early Literacy Measures are also available at http://www.aimsweb.com.

Early Literacy Skills

As opposed to screening approaches that seek to identify precursors of reading success or underlying causes of difficulties in learning to read, another approach is to screen students based on their attainment of early literacy skills. This approach follows research demonstrating that children who experience difficulties in acquiring early reading skills develop reading-related problems that are difficult to remediate (National Reading Panel, 2000). By closely monitoring the development of very early literacy related skills, these approaches can be effective in identifying students before significant reading failure occurs (Gijsel, Bosman, & Verhoeven, 2006; Kaminski & Good, 1996; Lyon et al., 2001) and may be more useful than formal classification approaches (McNamara, Scissons, & Dahleu, 2005). Davis, Lindo, and Compton (2007) call these skills, such as letter name knowledge, "measures of emerging print knowledge" (p. 3). For example, knowledge about letters, whether the names or the sounds, is a strong predictor of future reading achievement (Badian, 2000; Christensen, 2000).

Screening as a Dynamic Activity

Coyne, Kame'enui, and Simmons (2001) discuss the development of early screening programs to identify children at risk of reading failure. Essential to such efforts are setting benchmarks for expected progress and a dynamic approach to assessment that measures students' growth on critical early literacy skills as well as current status. Benchmarks of expected proficiency at a given level are developed through backward mapping. This process requires the collection of data that enables looking backward to see what levels of performance were achieved by children who went on to be successful on higher-order reading tasks at earlier points in time. Through this process, benchmarks are established that can help teachers in making decisions about what needs to be taught to particular students at particular points in time (Good, Simmons, & Kame'enui, 2001). Monitoring students' progress across time allows teachers to determine if a student who was considered at risk during an early screening is responding adequately to current instruction. An example of such measures, DIBELS, is described later. In addition, such measures are also available within many current reading curricula. Such procedures are incorporated in response to intervention models and will be discussed more thoroughly in Chap. 6. In addition, the rate of progress can provide another indicator of a student at risk for reading problems. Speece (2005) suggests that this type of dynamic information can be an important addition to the static information obtained through point-in-time screening.

Screening Measures

A variety of specific measures are available to screen for dyslexia at school entry. Table 4.5 provides a summary of the subtests within each of the measures described as follows.

Ready to Learn (Fawcett, Nicolson, & Lee, 2004)

Ready to Learn is designed for the assessment of children prior to, and at the beginning of, schooling (ages 3.6 to 6.5 years). The test contains 16 subtests that have been identified from the literature on dyslexia as being possible predictors of reading problems: rapid naming, bead threading, phonological discrimination, postural stability, balance, rhyme/alliteration, digit span, digit naming, letter naming, sound order, form matching, letter and shape copying, first letter sound, Corsi frog (a spatial memory task), and vocabulary. Ready to Learn is adapted from The Dyslexia Screening Test (DEST) originally developed in the United Kingdom. Like the DEST, Ready to Learn provides an "at-risk quotient" that combines a child's performance across the subtests. The Ready to Learn manual provides data on concurrent reliability and validity, but not predictive validity. However, Simpson and Everatt (2005) evaluated the ability of the DEST to predict reading outcomes 1 and 2 years after initial testing for 48 boys at school entry (mean age of 4.87). Within the DEST, sound order and rapid naming were better predictors of future reading outcomes than was the overall at-risk quotient. More importantly, the school-advministered measure of letter knowledge was more predictive than any of the DEST measures.

Table 4.5 Examples of screening tests

Test	Age range	Phonological Processing	Naming speed	Knowledge of letters/ print	Vocabulary	Other
Ready to learn	4.5–6.5 years	Yes	Yes	Yes	Yes	Memory, motor skills
TOPA	5.0–8.0 years	Yes				
TAAS	K to third grade	Yes				
Yopp-Singer	K to second grade	Yes				
TERA-3	3.5–8.5 years	Yes		Yes		Comprehension
DIBELS	K to third grade	Yes	Yes	Yes		

Test of Phonological Awareness – Second Edition: PLUS (Torgesen & Bryant, 2004)

The Test of Phonological Awareness – Second Edition: PLUS (TOPA-2+) is an individual- or group-administered test for use with children aged 5–8 years. There are two versions: kindergarten and early elementary. The tests are designed to "measure young children's ability to (a) isolate individual phonemes in spoken words and (b) understand the relationships between letters and phonemes in English" (http://www.proedinc.com/customer/productView.aspx?ID=860). Initial cost for the TOPA-2+ is $217.00 with additional test booklets costing $2.00 per booklet. Administration of the TOPA-2+, whether group or individual, takes about 30 min. The tasks on the kindergarten version ask the child to recognize and identify same and different beginning sounds for pictured objects and to identify which letter in a set of four corresponds to a phoneme said by the examiner. The elementary version requires the child to identify same and different final sounds in pictured objects and to spell pseudowords. Both versions were separately normed on samples of just over 1,000 students whose demographics matched 2001 US Bureau of the Census statistics. Internal consistency and test-retest reliability statistics range from 0.80 to 0.90. TOPA-2+ validity data includes a detailed description of, and rationale for, test/subtest content and format. Criterion and predictive validity found moderate associations with elements from the DIBELS and teacher ratings on the Learning Disabilities Diagnostic Inventory. Fenton (2005) reports that this measure "… is one of the few quick and easy-to-administer standardized norm-referenced indicators of early language skills that has a record of successful use and good evidence of test reliability and validity" (p. 11).

Test of Auditory Analysis Skills (Rosner, 1979)

The Test of Auditory Analysis Skills (TAAS) is a brief screening instrument designed to measure phonological awareness in young children. It contains 13 items that require the child to engage in increasingly complex segmentation activities (from segmenting compound words to separating consonant blends). Rosner provides suggested benchmarks for performance on the test from kindergarten through third grade. Rosner does not provide validity or reliability data on the test and Wilde, Goerss, and Wesler (2003) report that they were unable to find any pertinent reviews of the test. However, in their study, the TAAS administered during kindergarten demonstrated moderate correlation with reading assessment in first grade. The test is available in the 1979 Rosner book or through Academic Therapy Publications.

Yopp-Singer Test of Phoneme Segmentation (Yopp-Singer; Yopp, 1995)

The Yopp-Singer is a 22-item test of phoneme segmentation that is also designed for assessing the phonological processing abilities of young children. It requires the child to segment real words into their constituent sounds. It is free for use and available with directions at http://teams.lacoe.edu/reading/assessments/yopp.html. Yopp-Singer does not provide cut offs for expected performance. Wilde et al. (2003) report that the *Yopp Singer* did not correlate significantly with a standardized measure of first-grade reading.

Test of Early Reading Ability-3 (Rieid, Hresko, & Hammill, 2004)

The Test of Early Reading Ability-3 (TERA-3) is designed to measure the "mastery of early developing literacy skills" in children from 3 years 6 months to 8 years 6months. Three subtests are included that provide information on the child's knowledge of the alphabet and its uses, the conventions of print, and the child's ability to construct meaning from print. The TERA-3 was standardized on a sample of 875 school-aged children considered to be representative of the US population. Huff, Dancer, Evans, and Skoch (2006) evaluated an earlier version (the TERA-2) and found moderate correlations with reading related subtests of the *Woodcock Johnson Tests of Achievement 3* with a sample of preschool children. deFur's (2003) in her analysis of its technical adequacy comments: "...the technical development and analysis of the TERA-3 instills confidence that the test scores can be considered highly reliable and valid and that the authors have taken great care to address any inherent bias due to race, gender, ethnicity, SES, or disability" (p. 13). Finally, Smith (2003) concludes that the TERA-3 "...accomplishes its stated purposes, especially if used in conjunction with other assessments. Its strengths lie in the ease of administration, easy to use tables for scoring, and a clearly written examiner's manual" (p. 11). The TERA-3 takes approximately 30 min to administer with an initial cost of $250.00 and extra test booklets costing approximately $1.00 each.

Dynamic Indicators of Basic Early Literacy Skills (Good et al., 2003)

The DIBELS are a commonly used example of early literacy skills assessments that can be used both for screening and progress monitoring. Their use in progress monitoring and in helping to make diagnostic decisions about reading disability will be discussed further in Chap. 6. Published DIBELS measures (available for free download at http://dibels.uoregon.edu/or for purchase from Sopris West Publishers) provide performance benchmarks indicating whether a student is at high risk, some risk, or low risk on each measure. These benchmarks were established as part of research through the Early Childhood Research Institute on Measuring Growth and Development (Good et al., 2001).

The researchers correlated the DIBELS measures with important reading outcomes at later grades and then used scatterplot analysis to determine levels of performance at which students could be considered likely or unlikely to meet later outcomes based on the DIBELS scores. The DIBELS measures are designed to assess phonemic awareness, alphabetic understanding, accuracy and fluency with connected text, vocabulary development, and reading comprehension (Coyne & Harn, 2006). Phonemic awareness is assessed during kindergarten by two measures: Initial Sounds Fluency (ISF) and Phonemic Segmentation Fluency (PSF). The ISF requires two tasks of the child. The child is asked to identify which of a group of four pictured objects begins with the same sound an examiner says. The child is also asked to identify what sound a pictured object begins with. The measure takes 3 min to administer and the score is the number of initial sounds the child is able to identify in 1 min. PSF is administered beginning in winter of kindergarten and is predictive of future reading achievement (Kaminski & Good, 1996). In this task, the examiner presents a word orally and the student is asked to identify the constituent sounds in the word. Of importance is that scoring is based on the number of correct phoneme segments identified; thus, a child does not need to accurately identify all segments in the word to receive partial credit. The score is the number of correct segments identified per minute.

Another kindergarten assessment is letter name fluency (LNF). In this measure, the student identifies as many letters, presented in both upper and lower case, as possible in 1 min. This assessment is administered from the beginning of kindergarten through the beginning of first grade.

Like many screening instruments for young children, Hintze, Ryan, and Stoner (2003) found that DIBELS tend to have a high rate of false positives (identifying children as at risk who are not) though they were successful at identifying most students with reading problems when using risk status on the *Comprehensive Test of Phonological Processing* as the criterion for successful identification of students. It is important to acknowledge that the technical adequacy of DIBELS has been questioned (Burnsman, 2005). There is no technical manual and various online reports need to be examined to find information regarding the reliability and validity of these tests (and from such investigation it is found that not all tests offer this information). In his review of these measures, Shanahan (2005) concludes:

"Teachers need to treat the instructional recommendations derived from *DIBELS* as esti-
mates-useful approximations-as there are no data supporting the validity of the instructional categories used. The tests generally are valid indicators of reading ability, but the
ability of the test to correctly and accurately identify who would need additional help may
or may not be sound, though they look sensible." (p. 12)

As noted, DIBELS measures and similar early literacy measures are also
available at http://www.aimsweb.com (Early Literacy Skills).

Summary and Concluding Comments

The quest to find methods for identifying children at risk of dyslexia is an important endeavor and has received considerable research interest. One of the primary
problems in interpreting the research on predictors of reading disability is that
even when a factor has a high correlation it may still account for a relatively small
amount of a skill's variance. For example, phonological awareness tasks have
been proven to have a high correlation with reading and to be among the strongest
predictors in regression analysis. However, a correlation such as 0.7 between a
phonological processing task such as segmenting and later word reading means
that this skill accounts for only 49% of the variance in word reading. In other
words, despite fairly high correlation there is still considerable variation in word
reading skill that is not explained by differences in phonological processing.

Another issue is that prediction is not uniform across low and high levels of
performance in a task. As noted earlier, preschoolers who are good at rhyme are
likely to be good readers, but preschoolers who are not good at rhyme may or may
not be poor readers. This could be due to a number of factors. It might be that
rhyme or other phonological awareness tasks are truly not good predictors of later
reading. It could also be due to the vagaries of testing young children or to children's
interest in or exposure to rhyming activities. However, there is sufficient evidence
of the facilitative power of phonological awareness in developing reading skills to
consider it worthy of inclusion in screening of young children.

Among preschool children, the characteristics that tend to most consistently be
linked to poor reading outcomes are family history of dyslexia and/or global
language delays. Children with global language delays are at particular risk as they
do not possess skills in one aspect of language (such as semantics) to "bootstrap"
them in accommodating for weakness in other aspects (such as phonology). Studies
involving children at family risk of dyslexia are particularly relevant in highlighting
this interaction.

Once children begin schooling, it seems that assessing them on basic early
literacy skills is the most effective measurement. Across numerous studies, letter
knowledge measured at the beginning of or during kindergarten has been shown to
be the best predictor of success in mastering basic reading skills. This finding in
many ways seems to represent the obvious. If we want children to learn about the
alphabet and how it connects to spoken language, then testing them on their

knowledge of the alphabet seems the most sensible measure. However, one caveat is in regard to when such testing should be done. Testing children at the beginning of kindergarten will identify those children who are likely to not have problems in learning to read (true negatives), but will overidentify children at risk for learning to read (false positives) because many of the children with limited letter knowledge may simply have lacked exposure or interest. Therefore, letter knowledge as a screener for children at risk of dyslexia is most productive when administered at the middle of kindergarten after children have had an opportunity to learn about the alphabet.

Clearly, it is much easier to identify the characteristics of the child who is likely to be a successful reader than to identify the child who will struggle. Children who enter school with good language skills (i.e., phonologic, semantic, and syntactic skills), knowledge about the alphabet, and no family history of dyslexia are likely going to be successful readers. In addition, it is likely that a child with global language deficits, lack of alphabetic knowledge, and a family history of dyslexia is at high risk for reading disabilities. The difficulty lies in identifying those children who are at neither extreme, but have some of the characteristics that some of the time have been identified as predictors of reading disability.

Given these findings, the most worthwhile approach for school practitioners appears to be an awareness of the possible risk factors identified in this chapter coupled with an understanding of how these factors interact with each other to foster or impede reading development. With this knowledge, practitioners can be alert to children who possess a high number of risk factors and more closely monitor their progress in developing early literacy skills. Conversely, practitioners can institute the types of dynamic assessments of basic early literacy skills outlined and investigate the presence of risk factors for those children not demonstrating adequate progress and attainment of benchmarks. Those children not showing adequate progress, and particularly those exhibiting risk factors, could then be referred for more formal assessment.

Chapter 5
Diagnostic Assessment

As previously noted, the concept of dyslexia, or "congenital word blindness," has been with us since the late 1800s (Beaton, 2004). Given this fact, it is remarkable that this disorder is not specifically listed in either of the two most commonly used diagnostic systems available to us in the United States for categorizing learning disabilities, the *Individuals with Disabilities Act* (*IDEIA*, 2004) or the *Diagnostic and Statistical Manual of Mental Disorders-IV-Text Revision* (DSM-IV-TR: APA, 2000). In *IDEIA*, the closest to a diagnostic "fit" is the specific learning disability (SLD) category and *IDEIA*'s listing of dyslexia as a processing disorder (without an attempt to define it). In DSM-IV-TR, the term "reading disability" is used for what is commonly recognized as dyslexia. Consistent with the other books in this series, this chapter will delve further into how the DSM-IV-TR criteria and nomenclature are used for diagnostic purposes in regard to dyslexia. While these criteria might now be considered outdated (e.g., they still make use of an ability achievement discrepancy), knowledge of these criteria is important because this is the classification system most typically used by mental health professionals. A DSM-IV-TR diagnosis may also be required for insurance purposes and/or high stakes testing (e.g., SAT, GRE) accommodations. Chapter 6 will explore the *IDEIA* and how it relates to dyslexia, and it is in Chap. 6 that the most current and meaningful information about the identification of dyslexia can be found.

As pointed out by many (i.e., Brock, Jimerson, & Hansen, 2006), the diagnostic process is usually most comprehensive and successful when it makes use of a "team" approach, with each specialist screening and evaluating thoroughly within their area of expertise. Ideally, the diagnostic team includes a school psychologist, a special education teacher, a speech and language pathologist, an occupational therapist, and a pediatrician. Teams like these function best when they are well coordinated. However, there are a number of tests that cross professional boundaries, and the issue is not *who* should give a particular test, but that the *important* tests are given by a professional who can interpret them, and that all the information is consolidated to reduce inefficiency.

This chapter describes the diagnostic criteria for the three most likely DSM-IV-TR diagnoses available for a student with dyslexia: a reading disorder, a disorder of written expression, and a learning disorder not otherwise specified (LD-NOS). This chapter

C. Christo et al., *Identifying, Assessing, and Treating Dyslexia at School*,
DOI: 10.1007/978-0-387-88600-8_5, © Springer Science+Business Media, LLC 2009

also offers details regarding symptom onset, developmental course, associated features, gender-related features, and differential diagnoses. This information is followed with sections discussing the importance of taking developmental and family histories and using indirect or supporting observational criteria, as well as using more direct ways, usually with behavior rating scales, for assessing dyslexia. However, as just mentioned (and deserves to be reiterated) for this particular disorder, as will be discussed in Chap. 6, it is the psychoeducational assessment that is most critical to the diagnosis.

Reading Disorder

Diagnostic Criteria

The main focus of the DSM-IV-TR criteria is on significant and impairing reading failure that cannot be explained by developmental, intellectual, and/or sensory factors alone. Table 5.1 offers these criteria.

Symptom Onset

Some researchers (Lyytinen et al., 2004; Molfese, 2000; Molfese, Molfese, & Modglin, 2001) have found evidence that auditory event-related potential measurements in infancy can predict reading difficulties with symptom onset quite early. Others (Leppanen & Lyytinen, 1997; Scarborough, 1990) have documented early language deficits as predictive of later dyslexia. The body of evidence is fairly convincing that speech perception and/or phonological processing issues emerge early. There is often a mild delay in speaking first words and sentences, word pronunciation (e.g., "psghetti" for "spaghetti"), the ability to rhyme, and phonemic awareness, all of which can be considered early predictors and/or symptoms of dyslexia. In our intakes with parents of children we are assessing for

Table 5.1 DSM IV-TR: 315.00 diagnostic criteria for reading disorder (APA, 2000, p. 53)

Reading achievement, as measured by individually administered standardized tests of reading accuracy or comprehension, is substantially below that expected given the person's chronological age, measured intelligence, and age-appropriate education

The disturbance in Criterion A significantly interferes with academic achievement or activities of daily living that require reading skills

If a sensory deficit is present, the reading difficulties are in excess of those usually associated with it

Coding note: If a general medical (e.g., neurological) condition or sensory deficit is present, code the condition on Axis III

Reprinted with permission from the *Diagnostic and Statistical Manual of Mental Disorders*, Text Revision, Fourth Edition (Copyright 2000), American Psychiatric Association reading problems, we often ask if the child liked Dr. Suess or nursery rhymes. We do so as we and others (Bradley & Bryant, 1983; Lyytinen et al.) find that many youngsters with dyslexia have trouble with rhymes and word play, and do not enjoy these activities as much as their more language-proficient peers. However, in terms of specific reading-related activities, initial alphabet learning is one of the best predictors of later reading problems (Adams, 1990; Shaywitz, 2003).

Developmental Course

The vast majority of children with documented learning disabilities have reading problems (70–80%; Kirk & Elkins, 1975; Lyon & Moats, 1997). Although not all are dyslexic, most are. In addition, more than 17% of kindergarten to second-grade children in the US will encounter reading problems (National Reading Panel, 2000). Without intervention, 74% of the unsuccessful readers in third grade will continue to be unsuccessful readers in ninth grade (National Institute for Child Health and Human Development, 1999). As Moats (1999) has stated, "Dyslexia is a lifelong, intrinsic condition that is modified by instruction. The manifestations of dyslexia change as the individual grows and learns, although the underlying causal factors tend to be stable" (p. 3). Typical symptom development includes: initial language issues in preschool; alphabet learning difficulties in kindergarten; word identification, decoding, and spelling difficulties in kindergarten to second grade; reading fluency problems (which can create secondary reading comprehension problems) and written expression problems (especially with syntax and grammar) in third through sixth grades; and typically difficulties with second language learning in middle and/or high school (Shaywitz, 2003).

Associated Features

There are a number of social, behavioral, and socioemotional issues associated with dyslexia (Willcutt & Pennington, 2000a). Children and adolescents with dyslexia may not always be able to engage in the give and take of discussions due to language functioning and/or verbal working memory challenges and may therefore suffer socially. Students with dyslexia and/or learning disabilities tend to have a higher dropout rate, estimated at nearly 1.5 times the general population. Problems with reading and written expression can create issues later in life as well, especially with employment. This can be exacerbated if the adult with dyslexia is in a career where there is a lot of on-the-job learning and where significant amounts of independent reading are called for as part of the training process (APA, 2000).

In terms of behavioral and socioemotional issues, there are often secondary (some would say comorbid) anxiety, depression/dysthymia, and self-esteem issues (Cicci, 1995; Palombo, 2001; Ryan, 1994; Spekman, Goldberg, & Herman, 1993). Willcutt and Pennington (2000a, 2000b) found that there were significant correlations with a variety of diagnoses, but also that these comorbidities differ somewhat between males and females with reading disorders. They found that males with reading disorders had the following comorbidities: 40–45% AD/HD, almost 30% oppositional defiant disorder (ODD), a little over 20% conduct disorder (CD), 10% with depression, and a little over 20% with generalized anxiety disorder (GAD). Females with reading disorders had the following comorbidities: between 15 and 20% had AD/HD, about 10% had ODD, about 5% had CD, a little over 20% had depression, and almost 25% had GAD. These behavioral and socioemotional issues can often lead to challenges with cooperation and motivation that then have to be given treatment priority so as to allow the students to begin to meaningfully re-engage with academics.

Gender-Related Issues

The DSM-IV-TR (APA, 2000) states that "from 60 to 80% of individuals diagnosed with reading disorders are males" (p. 52). Although they also state that this number may be inflated by referral biases, they do not update what is now known about gender and dyslexia. In particular, during the 1990s, research revealed that when psychometric testing and/or screening is used on all boys and girls without referrals from school personnel, the incidence rates are nearly equal, with perhaps a slight increase of boys over girls, which tends to lack statistical significance (Flynn & Childs, 1994; Shaywitz, Shaywitz, Fletcher, & Escobar, 1990; Wadsworth, DeFries, Stevenson, Gilger, & Pennington, 1992). However, as discussed in Chap. 4, some authors argue that boys do have a higher incidence of dyslexia than girls though not at the rates seen in school-identified populations and suggested in DSM-IV-TR.

Differential Diagnosis

Traditionally, the major differential diagnoses for dyslexia are a more global speech and language disorder, mental retardation, sensory deficits, or lack of opportunity to learn (APA, 2000). Within the conceptual framework of the DSM-IV-TR diagnostic system, these rule outs would stay the same *because* it still utilizes a discrepancy model, whereby a language disorder and mental retardation can be ruled out as part of a comprehensive cognitive and educational battery. However, as indicated later, other ways of conceptualizing/diagnosing *dyslexia* also fit with what is known.

Disorder of Written Expression

As detailed in Table 5.2, a disorder of written expression is again based on a discrepancy model with the results of individually administered standardized tests of written expression being significantly different from IQ or chronological age expectations. In addition, the diagnosis of written expression in the DSM-IV-TR allows for

Table 5.2 DSM IV-TR: 315.2 diagnostic criteria for a disorder of written expression (APA, 2000, p. 56)

Writing skills, as measured by individually administered standardized tests (or functional assessments of writing skills), are substantially below those expected given the person's chronological age, measured intelligence, and age-appropriate education

The disturbance in Criterion A significantly interferes with academic achievement or activities of daily living that require the composition of written texts (e.g., writing grammatically correct sentences and organized paragraphs)

If a sensory deficit is present, the difficulties in writing skills are in excess of those usually associated with it

Coding note: If a general medical (e.g., neurological) condition or sensory deficit is present, code the condition on Axis III

Reprinted with permission from the *Diagnostic and Statistical Manual of Mental Disorders*, Text Revision, Fourth Edition (Copyright 2000), American Psychiatric Association

a *functional* assessment of writing skill. The DSM-IV-TR points out that a functional assessment can be more important in the area of written expression because there are fewer available tests of written expression, and these tests are less well developed than available reading and math tests. Further, the existing written expression tests rarely capture all the demands of written expression especially at the middle and high school levels (APA, 2000).

It is also important to remember that "written language is by far the most difficult academic subject, requiring virtually every part of the brain to work concertedly toward a final product" (Hale & Fiorello, 2004, p. 237). Therefore, it is likely that students with dyslexia, AD/HD, and/or nonverbal learning disorders (and likely all students who have some other learning issues) will also have difficulties with written expression, but for *different* reasons.

Symptom Onset

If the cause of the writing problem is handwriting, or what is sometimes referred to as *dysgraphia*, then symptoms are often first seen before kindergarten as a fine motor or visual motor integration problem (Berninger & Graham, 1998). However, for students with dyslexia, what is most predictable is that in late kindergarten through second grade, spelling problems emerge (Ehri, 1992a, 1992b, 2000; Moats, 2000). Typically for students with dyslexia, the types of writing difficulties they manifest are primarily in the areas of structure, syntax, grammar, and often fluency (Hale & Fiorello, 2004).

Developmental Course

As mentioned earlier, among students with dyslexia, writing difficulties typically arise during the early elementary years. Isaacson (1996) suggests that in most cases these early writing difficulties continue to exist as students progress through their schooling. This is supported by national data that suggest the incidence of written expression disorders among school-aged youth is at least as high as for reading disorders (Hallahan & Kauffman, 2000; Howell & Nolet, 2000) and that 16% of fourth graders, 16% of eighth graders, and 22% of twelfth graders were performing at below the basic level for written expression as measured by group standardized tests (National Center for Education Statistics, 1998).

Although these difficulties do not go away, with appropriate intervention, they can at least be somewhat ameliorated. A recent meta-analysis found three areas that were important areas of instruction and were found to improve writing skills. These areas were explicit instruction in the writing process (e.g., planning, organization, writing, editing, and revising), explicit instruction in the structure of the writing process (e.g., promoting the recognition of the recurring structures and patterns involved), and finally incorporating some variation of guided feedback whereby students received monitoring and feedback from peers and/or teachers in an ongoing fashion with rewrites (Gersten & Baker, 2001).

Associated Features

Clearly, among students with dyslexia the most commonly associated features are reading difficulties. It is likely that there are other comorbidities, probably much like that found among students with reading disorders, with the exception of a developmental coordination disorder source as mentioned in the DSM-IV-TR.

Gender-Related Features

A review of the *PsycInfo* research database identified no studies investigating gender differences and disorders of written expression and none is mentioned in the DSM-IV-TR. However, given what we know about the dyslexia research, we can hypothesize that in a referred population males would be over-represented, while in a nonreferred population incidence rates are likely to be more equal.

Differential Diagnosis

Other than developmental coordination disorder (DSM-IV-TR: 315.4), the differential diagnoses would be the same as with reading disorders.

Learning Disorder Not Otherwise Specified

This disorder is added because it is somewhat different than the two described earlier and can be useful at times for some students, especially those needing accommodations in high school or college. Table 5.3 presents these diagnostic criteria. Here, the discrepancy criterion does not need to be met if there is sufficient evidence of impairment over multiple categories. One way that this is fairly common for many students with dyslexia relates to reading fluency. A student with a fluency discrepancy alone will not meet discrepancy criteria; however, any timed tests that require reading will be impacted by a fluency disorder. When this occurs, LD-NOS can be applied to justify the appropriate testing accommodations. Other than this difference, the remainder of the areas covered earlier can be applied to LD-NOS.

Developmental, Health, and Family History

A developmental and health history should be considered an essential part of any diagnostic and/or psychoeducational evaluation as it is important for all school psychologists to understand the context within which a child has developed (Hale & Fiorello, 2004; Teeter & Semrud-Clikeman, 1997). In addition to individually developed history forms (see Fig. 5.1 for an example developed by the third author), published formats include the *Behavioral Assessment System for Children* (2nd ed.; BASC; Reynolds & Kamphaus, 2004) as well as a number of tests that allow reproduction of forms (e.g., NEPSY-II; Korkman, Kirk, & Kemp, 2007).

Perinatal Risk Factors

For developmental dyslexia no pre-, peri-, or postnatal factors have been causally linked to developmental dyslexia other than the aforementioned genetic contributions. However, in terms of postnatal risk factors, there is a significant

Table 5.3 DSM IV-TR: 315.9 diagnostic criteria for learning disorder not otherwise specified (APA, 2000, p. 56)

This category is for disorders in learning that do not meet criteria for any specific learning disorder. This category might include problems in all three areas (reading, mathematics, written expression) that together significantly interfere with academic achievement even though performance on tests measuring each individual skill is not substantially below that expected given the person's chronological age, measured intelligence, and age-appropriate education

Reprinted with permission from the *Diagnostic and Statistical Manual of Mental Disorders*, Text Revision, Fourth Edition (Copyright 2000), American Psychiatric Association

COLLEGE OF EDUCATION
DEPARTMENT OF SPECIAL EDUCATION, REHABILITATION
AND SCHOOL PSYCHOLOGY

CALIFORNIA STATE UNIVERSITY,
SACRAMENTO

School Psychology Diagnostic Clinic
6000 J Street
Sacramento, California 95819-6079

DYSLEXIA DIAGNOSTIC EVALUATION
HEALTH, FAMILY, DEVELOPMENTAL, & BEHAVIORAL HISTORY INTERVIEW FORM

Child's Name: _____   Birth date: _____
School: _____   Grade: _____
Parent(s): _____   E-mail: _____
Home phone: _____   Alt. Phone: _____
Languages spoken in the home: _____
Siblings and their ages: _____
Other adults living in the home: _____

Number of books in the home (circle):	None	Several (< 20)	Many (20+)	Hundreds
Times per week the child is read to (circle):	Never	1-2 days	3-5 days	6-7 days

Referring concern: _____
_____
_____
_____
_____
_____

At what age and/or grade did the referring concerns first emerge? _____

Health History (Perinatal Factors)

1. General obstetric status (circle one):   Optimal   Adequate   Poor
                                               Describe: _____
                                               _____
                                               _____
                                               _____

2. Alcohol exposure during pregnancy (circle): YES   NO   If YES answer the following:
    a.   How often did mother drink?   Every day   Once a week   Rarely
    b.   How much did mother drink?   Just a little One drink   Several drinks
    c.   When during pregnancy did
         mother drink?   1st trimester 2nd Trimester 3rd trimester

3. Drug exposure during pregnancy (circle): YES   NO   If YES answer the following:
    a.   What drugs were taken?   List: _____
                                            _____
                                            _____
                                            _____

    b.   When during pregnancy were
         drugs taken?   1st trimester 2nd Trimester 3rd trimester

Fig. 5.1 (continued)

Health History (Perinatal Factors, continued)

4. Complications during delivery (circle)?   YES   NO   If YES describe:
   Describe: _____
   _____
   _____
   _____

5. Birth weight (list):   _____lbs.   _____oz.

Health History (Infancy and childhood)

6. Illnesses
   (Describe/List when illness occurred)?   _____
                                               _____
                                               _____

7. Chronic ear infections   YES   NO   If YES answer the following:
   a.   When did they occur?   _____ months to _____ months
   b.   How often did they occur?   _____ per month (or) _____ per year
   c.   Were tubes placed?   YES   NO   When?_____
   d.   Was there hearing loss?   YES   NO   If YES describe
                                               _____
                                               _____

8. Other Medical Diagnoses/Issues (circle):   High fevers   Head trauma
                                               Fetal alcohol syndrome   Epilepsy
                                               Lead poisoning   Mental retardation
                                               Immune dysfunction   Thyroid problems
                                               Arthritis   Cerebral palsy
                                               Allergy history   Gastrointestinal symptoms
                                               Hydrocephalus   Prolong hospitalizations
                                               Other (list): _____
                                               _____
                                               _____

9. Suspected vision loss   YES   NO   If YES describe reasons for
                                               concern: _____
                                               _____
                                               _____

10. Suspected hearing loss   YES   NO   If YES describe reasons for
                                               concern: _____
                                               _____
                                               _____

11. Vision Screening (list):   Date: _____   Near 20/____   Far 20/____

12. Hearing Screening (list):   Date: _____   Result: _____

Fig. 5.1 (continued)

Family History

13. Parent with dyslexia (circle)?   YES   NO

14. Parent with learning disability(ies; circle)?   YES   NO

15. Family members with dyslexia (circle)?   YES   NO   If YES answer the following:
    a.   Relationship to child (list):   _____
    b.   An identical twin?   YES   NO

16. Family members with learning disability   YES   NO   If YES answer the following:
(ies; circle)?
    a.   Relationship to child (list):   _____
    b.   An identical twin?   YES   NO

17. Health/developmental problems
among family members?   Describe: _____
    _____
    _____
    _____

18. Maternal educational attainment
(circle)?   No High School   Some High School
                                      High School Grad.   Some College
                                      College Grad.   Some Graduate School
                                      Degree(s, List): _____

19. Paternal educational attainment
(circle)?   No High School   Some High School
                                        High School Grad.   Some College
                                      College Grad.   Some Graduate School
                                      Degree(s, List): _____

Developmental History

20. Age major milestones were obtained   First word   _____months
(list)?   Sentences   _____months
                                        Stands alone   _____months
                                        First steps   _____months
                                        Walks alone   _____months

Fig. 5.1 (continued)

Diagnostic History

21. Speech/Articulation disorders   YES   NO
      a.   Type(s) of disorder (list):   _____
      b.   Type(s) of treatment (list):   _____
      c.   Duration of treatment (list):   _____

22. Language disorders   YES   NO
      a.   Type(s) of disorder (list):   _____
      b.   Type(s) of treatment (list):   _____
      c.   Duration of treatment (list):   _____

23. Central Auditory Processing difficulties   YES   NO
      a.   Type(s) of treatment (list):   _____
      b.   Duration of treatment (list):   _____

24. AD/HD   YES   NO
      a.   Type(s) of disorder (list):   _____
      b.   Type(s) of treatment (list):   _____
      c.   Duration of treatment (list):   _____

25. Other diagnoses (list)   _____
                                           _____
                                         _____
                                         _____

School History

26. Number of schools attended (list)   _____

27. School attendance history (describe)   _____
                                         _____

28. Prior special education services?   YES   NO

29. Educational interventions (describe)   _____
                                         _____
                                         _____
                                         _____

Reading Related Behavioral History[1]

30. Infant (birth to 18 months)
        Focused eyes on an object   YES   NO
        Reached for and held books   YES   NO
        Held head steady and sat without support   YES   NO
        Pointed with one finger at an object   YES   NO
        Turned board pages, several at a time   YES   NO
        Looked at pictures   YES   NO
        Vocalized at, patted, and pointed to pages/pictures   YES   NO
        Turned books right side up   YES   NO
        Gave books to an adult to read   YES   NO

Fig. 5.1 (continued)

31. Toddler (18 months to 3 years)

Turned board pages, one at a time	YES	NO
Carried books	YES	NO
Named familiar pictures	YES	NO
Filled in words in familiar stories	YES	NO
Pretended to read to others	YES	NO
Recited parts of well-known stories	YES	NO
Learned to handle paper pages	YES	NO
Found favorite pictures in books	YES	NO
Related text to pictures	YES	NO
Protested when words in a familiar story were read wrong	YES	NO
Read familiar books to self	YES	NO
Named family member pictures	YES	NO
Recognized familiar signs (e.g., fast food restaurants)	YES	NO

32. Preschool (3 to 5 years)

Was able to handle/manipulate books	YES	NO
Turned paper pages, one at a time	YES	NO
Listened to longer stories	YES	NO
Was able to retell a familiar story	YES	NO
Understood what text is	YES	NO
Moved finger along text	YES	NO
"Wrote" name	YES	NO
Was able to pronounce words without problem (i.e., no baby talk)	YES	NO
Had no difficulty finding the right word in speech	YES	NO
Was able to rhyme words	YES	NO
Learned common nursery rhymes (e.g., "Jack and Jill")	YES	NO
Learned letters in own name	YES	NO
Was learning numbers/letters	YES	NO
Noticed if parents skipped a word while reading	YES	NO
Was able to name shapes and colors	YES	NO
Was able to recognize own name in print	YES	NO
Was able to repeat the alphabet without the "ABC" song	YES	NO

33. Kindergarten and First Grade (6 to 7 years)

Learned letter sound associations	YES	NO
Did not confuse basic words (e.g., run and eat)	YES	NO
Learned that words come apart (e.g., "batboy" = "bat" and "boy")	YES	NO
Learned that words come apart (e.g., "bat" = "b" "aaa" "t")	YES	NO
Reading errors were phonetic (e.g., "bat"="bait," not "bat"="goat")	YES	NO
Read common one-syllable words (e.g., mat, cat, sat)	YES	NO
Enjoyed reading (i.e., no complaints about it being hard)	YES	NO

34. Second Grade and Beyond (8 years and older)

Was able to pronounce long, unfamiliar, complicated words	YES	NO
Speech was fluent (e.g., no pauses, hesitations, or a lot of "um's")	YES	NO
Language was precise (e.g., avoids "stuff" instead of object names)	YES	NO
Was able to "find" words easily when speaking	YES	NO
Needed little time to summon an oral response	YES	NO
Was able to quickly remember dates, names, phone numbers, etc.	YES	NO
Was able to read/sound out new and unfamiliar words	YES	NO

Fig. 5.1 (continued)

Could describe how to read new and unfamiliar words	YES	NO
Was able to read "function" words (e.g., "that" "an" "in")	YES	NO
Was able to read/sound out multi-syllable words	YES	NO
Enjoyed reading and has no fear of reading out loud	YES	NO
Oral reading became fluent (not slow and tiring)	YES	NO
Oral reading included inflections and sounds	YES	NO
Did well on multiple choice tests	YES	NO
Ability to read single words was as strong as passage comprehension	YES	NO
Finished tests on time	YES	NO
Spelling errors were close to true spelling	YES	NO
Was able to read math word problems	YES	NO
Was able to finish homework in a timely fashion	YES	NO
Read for pleasure	YES	NO
Was able to learn a foreign language	YES	NO
Did not substitute words unable to pronounce with words that had the same meaning (e.g., "car" for "automobile")	YES	NO

Fig. 5.1 This figure offers a history form that includes items that have been suggested to be associated with the development of dyslexia

amount of evidence supporting the notion that early exposure to language and print does contribute to reading skills, and that without sufficient exposure to language and being read to, reading skills are likely to lag (e.g., Cunningham & Stanovich, 1990, 1991, 1993). As mentioned in other parts of this book, phonological development, currently considered the "core deficit" by most in the field, can be impacted by lack of exposure or environmental factors, although for a "true" dyslexic the genetic predisposition, or the inheritability factor associated with it, is usually thought to be important and more so than for the "garden variety" poor reader (Stanovich, 1988).

Another postnatal risk factor often cited and researched in terms of its relationship to reading disorders, again not necessarily dyslexia per se, is otitis media (OM; a middle ear inflammation). Earlier research on this childhood condition was complicated by methodology, clinical vs. epidemiological approaches, and reliability of measures (e.g., Alho, 1990; Bishop & Edmundson, 1987; Eimas & Clarkson, 1986). However, some things are clear. It is known that about 70% of all children experience acute otitis media during the first three years of life. During the course of the disease, liquid builds in the middle ear. Whether this liquid/condition, often referred to as otitis media with effusion (OME), is a reaction to the infection or to an immature Eustachian tube is not clear. Of the 70% that contract OM about 20% maintain OME for up to 2 months after the acute phase and about 10% maintain it for up to 3 months after the acute phase (Bluestone & Klein, 2001; Roush, 2001). This fluid can impede normal sound wave transmission. As noted in Chap. 4, the initial phase of "fine tuning" the phonology of a specific language/culture is ages 6 to 18 months, and researchers have found that frequent and/or severe cases of OME can impact the development of phonological awareness (e.g., Menyuk, 1986; Mody, Schwartz, Gravel, & Ruben, 1999; Nittrouer, 1995). Interestingly, even though this part is fairly well supported, the research on the impact of OME on reading is less conclusive (e.g., Roberts et al., 2000; Wallace & Hooper, 1997). Although all this suggests that there may be multiple streams that flow into a reading disorder, most of it implicates phonological development which, regardless of its cause, also has some relatively effective treatments.

Developmental Milestones

The diagnostic evaluation should collect information on all basic areas of early development. In particular, when reading problems are a symptom, questions should be asked regarding attainment of major language milestones as well as unusual variations in such development (e.g., phonemic confusion, retrieval problems, pronunciation difficulties, remembering names, following directions). Questions should be asked about early language and educational experiences (Hale & Fiorello, 2004; Wilkins & Garside, 1993). When a school-aged student is being evaluated, contacting previous preschool and school-aged teachers might yield additional useful information regarding exposure to language and print as well as reading interventions previously tried with the student.

Medical and Diagnostic History

As mentioned earlier, knowledge about number and severity of chronic ear infections is important. To rule out other traumatic origins of reading problems, questions should be asked about high and/or extended fevers, traumatic head injuries, any prolonged hospitalizations, or long lapses in school attendance. Included in this would also be questions regarding the child's treatment and diagnostic history (Deisinger, 2001). Practitioners should seek information as to whether the child has been diagnosed and/or treated for speech or language disorders, evaluated or diagnosed with AD/HD, been evaluated for or diagnosed with a Central Auditory Processing Disorder (National Institute on Deafness and Other Communication Disorders, 2004), or any other relevant hearing or language-based issues.

Family History

Finally, a family history of any reading, language, spelling, or second language acquisition problems would be supportive of a diagnosis of dyslexia. As previously mentioned, dyslexia is heritable (e.g., DeFries, Fulker & LaBuda, 1987; Pennington et al. 1991). When exploring this history with parents, it is crucial to avoid this becoming a genetic "blame game." However, in our experience, when we have good rapport with the parents we often find that parents report early reading problems as the evaluation of the child unfolds.

Indirect Assessment

The diagnostic assessment involves obtaining data from caregivers (e.g., parents/ guardians and teachers) about the child being assessed. It allows the evaluator to capture "real world" or contextualized behavior without having to observe it, which at times could be a helpful and cost-effective procedure. However, it is important to acknowledge the subjective nature of indirect assessment. On some occasions, caregivers have biased and/or inaccurate views of a child's behavior (Goin & Myers, 2004). Thus, more direct assessment (to be discussed in Chap. 6) is also an important element of any diagnostic assessment and, for dyslexia, probably the most important.

Indirect assessment may be further divided into less formal and more formal/ standardized procedures. In informal procedures, the mental health professional can utilize either or both naturalistic and/or systematic approaches. These approaches have been found to be the most frequently used tools by school psychologists (Wilson & Reschley, 1996). However, given that dyslexia is most often considered a "hidden disability," one has to be very careful about how to use these observational data (i.e., we do not want to intervene on the *reaction* to reading failure, as with reduced cooperation, if we have missed the *cause* of failure, poor phonological and/or reading skills).

In terms of a more formalized approach to observations, the only instrument identified is the *Dyslexia Screening Instrument* (DSI: Nicolson & Fawcett, 2004). This rating scale consists of 33 statements believed to be associated with reading problems. A teacher rates the student on a 5-point Likert scale across all 33 items from 1 = *never exhibits* to 5 = *always exhibits*. When entered into the scoring program, the software provides a Pass, Fail, or Inconclusive classification on the rated student; Pass indicating no concerns, Fail indicating significant concerns, and Inconclusive suggesting more information needs to be gathered. Reliability and validity measures for the DSI are adequate. In a separate study (Sofie & Riccio, 2002), it was found that the DSI had moderate correlations with measures of reading, in the $r = 0.6$ range, and moderate correlations with measures of phonological processing, from $r = 0.4$ to $r = 0.6$. These results support the notion that the DSI could be useful as part of the initial evaluation of students for reading disorders; however, perhaps the more interesting data to collect would have been to see whether the accurate identification rate for students with reading problems would have been greatly enhanced by the DSI as opposed to just having the teachers sort their students to each of the three categories.

Concluding Comments

As previously mentioned, since up to 80% (Lyon et al., 2001) of students with a
SLD are likely to have a reading disorder, all mental health professionals will need
to be prepared to understand dyslexia and to help school personnel think about
appropriate treatments for dyslexia. This chapter identified and examined some of
the issues relevant to the DSM-IV-TR diagnosis of this disorder. While we do not
recommend use of this classification framework as the primary method of diagnosing
dyslexia (and in fact suggest that Chap. 6 will provide more appropriate guidance
on this topic), we also acknowledge that this is the framework most commonly used
by mental health professionals in the US and that not having a diagnostic or eligibility system to be more specific about what dyslexia is, is a distinct disadvantage.
Thus, we hope this chapter has been helpful in understanding issues relevant to this
common diagnostic system.

We also recognize that some school districts are hesitant to practice outside our
educational code and so are reluctant to use the term "dyslexia" when talking with
school personnel and parents about a particular student. However, it has also been
our experience that many parents, especially since the publication of Sally
Shaywitz's (2003) book on dyslexia, have become more informed about this
disorder and become more knowledgeable about its treatment. We have also found
that failing to dialogue about this with the parents with whom we work can be
problematic and place a strain on or break the rapport we need to continue to work
with these parents. Having informed school personnel *and* informed parents is an
asset when trying to plan for and to help children with dyslexia.

Chapter 6
Psychoeducational Assessment

The primary purpose of a school-based assessment for a child suspected of having dyslexia is to provide information useful in educational planning. This may include information relevant to special education eligibility as well as information that helps teams better understand children and their processing, and decide on the most appropriate instructional interventions. Chapter 5 discussed the diagnosis of dyslexia and related academic disorders primarily in the context of DSM-IV-TR. This chapter will address diagnosis in relation to the need for special education services (*IDEIA* eligibility) and the components of an evaluation that are most pertinent to educational planning. Many school practitioners are uncomfortable making a determination that a child has "dyslexia"; however, we would argue that a well-trained school psychologist with the requisite knowledge of this disorder is more than capable of determining whether a child's cognitive and academic profile fits the definition of dyslexia as currently defined (Lyon, Shaywitz, & Shaywitz, 2003). The diagnosis of dyslexia per se may not be critical to educational planning, provided that the information that would normally be gathered in such a diagnosis is available to a team in their intervention planning process. However, the diagnosis may help both the school and parents to better understand and plan for a student's educational experiences. Dyslexia is a lifelong condition; thus, it is important for parents and students to understand the possible long-term impacts of dyslexia.

Special Education Eligibility: Overview of Federal Regulations

As noted in Chap. 1, the definition of a learning disability has remained the same in *IDEIA* (2004) as it was in the 1997 reauthorization of the law and its subsequent regulations. 34 CFR § 300.309 of the *IDEIA* 2004 Code of Federal Regulations (CFR; U.S. Department of Education, 2006) addresses eligibility for special education as a child with a specific learning disability (SLD). This section has three subclauses: (a), (b), and (c). Section 300.309(a) includes three criteria for SLD consideration (a) low achievement in one of eight specified areas; (b) using either (1) a response-to-intervention (RTI) approach or (2) pattern of strengths and weaknesses to identify a child who may have a SLD; and (c) the exclusionary factors. Section 300.309(b)

C. Christo et al., *Identifying, Assessing, and Treating Dyslexia at School*,
DOI: 10.1007/978-0-387-88600-8_6, © Springer Science+Business Media, LLC 2009

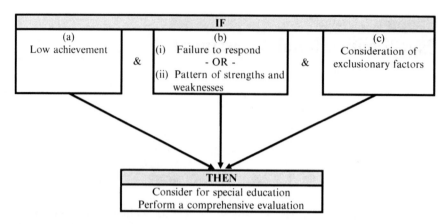

Fig. 6.1 SLD eligibility factors in *IDEIA* (2004) (U.S. Department of Education, 2006, § 300.309(a)(b)(c)

addresses the need to assure that a child has had appropriate instruction (this is in addition to exclusionary factors in 300.309[a][3]) and that progress has been documented. Finally, section 300.309(c) states that if these conditions are met, then the child needs to be referred for an evaluation to determine if they qualify as a child with a SLD and needs special education. Figure 6.1 graphically represents the criteria in each of the subsections (a) through (c). Each of these sections will be further explained later. However, before discussing *IDEIA* eligibility, we will present a brief overview of RTI approaches to instruction and intervention. This approach has been brought to the attention of educators to a significant degree by references to it in *IDEIA*.

Response-to-Intervention Models

RTI refers to the practice of providing "high quality instruction and interventions matched to student need, monitoring progress frequently to make decisions about changes in instruction or goals and applying child response data to important educational decisions" (National Association of State Directors of Special Education [NASDSE], 2007, p. 3). In schools implementing RTI models, a tiered system of interventions is provided to students identified as either not meeting early benchmarks or not making expected levels of progress as a result of an intervention targeting a specified academic deficit. Within this model, lack of response to high-quality instruction or intervention that works for most students indicates the need for a more intensive or broader intervention and ultimately may indicate the need for a comprehensive evaluation and special education consideration. RTI approaches are referred to in *IDEIA* (2004) as one process for determining whether a child should be referred for a comprehensive evaluation to determine need and eligibility (U.S. Department of

Education, 2006, 34 CFR § 300.309[a][2]) for special education services as a student with a SLD. RTI approaches rest on two solid research bases (a) findings supporting the effectiveness of early intervening for children experiencing delays in reading development and (b) findings regarding the usefulness of formative progress monitoring of key academic skills. It is important to note that the results of an RTI process do not themselves constitute sufficient evidence to deem a child eligible for, and in need of, special education services. However, the data gathered during an RTI process would play an important part in a comprehensive evaluation.

Common features of RTI models include high-quality, evidence-based instruction and intervention, methods for assuring fidelity in the implementation of interventions, universal screening of all children to identify those at risk of academic problems, early intervention, and progress monitoring of students receiving intervention services (Bender & Shores, 2007; Fuchs, 2004; Fuchs & Fuchs, 2006; Mellard & Johnson, 2008; NASDSE, 2007). An RTI model provides a framework for a tiered approach to providing interventions of varying levels of intensity to struggling students. These models may have from 3–5 levels of interventions. Within a typical three-tiered RTI model, the first tier represents classroom instruction. The RTI model assumes that the classroom curriculum is effective for most students and that within the curriculum there are methods for differentiating the instruction according to student need. The second tier consists of more intensive interventions for those students not responding appropriately to first tier instruction. Intensity can be increased through smaller instructional groups, more focused instruction (possibly with a supplemental program), or more instructional time. In some models, the third tier represents the types of interventions that are more typical of special education and are characterized by greater intensity of instruction achieved through individualized focus, remedial curriculum, or more time.

Data that can be expected to result from an RTI approach consist at minimum of information on what specific instructional methods and intervention strategies were used, how effective these methods were with other students, how the student is progressing on key academic indicators of literacy, where the student performs in relation to peers, and the amount of progress that the student displays in response to the instruction and intervention utilized. The RTI process provides valuable information about the student's instructional history, that is useful both in eligibility decisions and in future educational planning. In addition, diagnostic information (such as behavior rating scales and phonological processing measures) may have been collected as a result of failure to respond, and this information will also become part of the comprehensive evaluation. It is beyond the scope of this chapter to discuss RTI models in depth. The reader is referred to http://www.nrcld.org/topics/rti.html and *Handbook of Response to Intervention* (Jimerson, Burns, & VanDerHeyden, 2007) for further information on RTI approaches.

Following are specifics about the components of SLD criteria in the federal regulations, and the types of information that both traditional measures and an RTI process can provide. It is also important to note that each state will interpret these guidelines in its own manner. Therefore, the relevancy of the information included here is subject to interpretation within the guidelines of each reader's state regulations.

Low Achievement

34 CFR § Section 300.309(a)(1) refers to low achievement as the first criterion. This section states:

> "The child does not achieve adequately for the child's age or to meet State-approved grade-level standards in one or more of the following areas, when provided with learning experiences and instruction appropriate for the child's age or State-approved grade-level standards:
>
>   (i)   Oral expression.
>   (ii)   Listening comprehension.
>   (iii) Written expression.
>   (iv) Basic reading skill.
>   (v)   Reading fluency skills.
>   (vi) Reading comprehension.
>   (vii) Mathematics calculation.
>   (viii) Mathematics problem solving." (U.S. Department of Education, 2006, p. 46786)

Low achievement is present in most definitions of learning disability (Flanagan, Ortiz, Alfonso, & Dynda, 2006). In the U.S. Department of Education (2006) regulations, the standard for comparison of achievement is age or state-level standards. The benchmark and progress-monitoring data collected through an RTI process can provide information as to whether a student is consistently meeting academic benchmarks at a rate similar to peers or at a rate that indicates the student will meet state-level standards. RTI data also provide information relevant to the appropriateness of the instruction. For example, if students similar to the target student are making adequate progress, then that is a good indication of the quality of instruction.

Low achievement might also be evidenced through performance on state perform-ance standards: for example, scores below the proficient level. District benchmark assessments are another source of information on performance. Classroom grades as well as performance on curriculum-embedded measures may further provide evidence of low achievement. We recommend that when making eligibility decisions, perfor-mance on traditional nationally normed achievement tests also be included in the decision-making process.

Lack of Progress or Pattern of Strengths and Weaknesses

34 CFR § 300.309(a)(2) provides two different options for meeting the second crite-rion. These options are (a) lack of progress and (b) pattern of strengths and weaknesses.

Lack of Progress

Section 300.309(a)(2)(i) reads as follows:

"The child does not make sufficient progress to meet age or State approved grade-level stand-ards in one or more of the areas identified in paragraph (a)(1) of this section when using a process based on the child's response to scientific, research-based intervention." (U.S. Department of Education, 2006, p. 46786)

The "process" referred to in this section is generally thought of as an RTI process. Two important elements in any RTI process are the use of instructional and intervention techniques that have a research base behind them and the use of a measure that monitors short-term progress on key academic indicators. Curriculum-Based Measurement (CBM) is the type of assessment most commonly suggested for use in an RTI process. Instructional and intervention programs with a research base will be discussed in Chap. 7. Within the RTI process referred to in this section, a student's rate of RTI, as well as current level of performance, determine whether the student needs more intensive intervention. Progress-monitoring data, such as those available through CBM, provide a comparison between baseline, rate of growth, and current level of performance for the student and peers as well as rate of growth toward state-approved grade-level standards in response to these interventions. Progress-monitoring data generated through the RTI process will provide a comparison of the target student's progress with other students and toward established benchmarks. To meet this criterion, the rate of progress should be substantially discrepant from that of other students. It also provides information relevant to whether the intervention or instruction was successful with most students. The implication is that if a student does not respond adequately to instruction that is generally effective, then the child may have a learning disability and be in need of special education services.

The early literacy measures discussed in Chap. 4 (e.g., DIBELS; Good et al., 2003; *AIMSWeb Early Literacy Measures*) are particularly useful in an RTI model as they provide tools for monitoring progress of the development of critical early literacy skills. These skills include phonological processing, letter knowledge, and phonics. Thus, schools can determine which students are making adequate progress on these key skills before more formal reading measures are used. In addition, if schools use the same measures for both benchmarking all students and for progress monitoring, it is very easy to monitor progress toward benchmarks of those students receiving interventions.

Important questions regarding the use of student RTI and instruction include set-ting criteria for both benchmarks and adequate level of response (Fuchs, Fuchs, & Compton, 2004). Currently, there are potential benchmarks for measures such as the early literacy measures (see http://dibels.uoregon.edu;http://www.edformation.com; Hall, 2006). However, these benchmarks are based on a national database and may not reflect a student's local peer group. It is also important to note that the national database consists of those using the measures: it is not necessarily a demographically representative sample.

In addition to benchmarks, expectations for rate of growth on key early literacy measures have also been developed (Deno, Fuchs, Marston, & Shin, 2001; Fuchs & Fuchs, 2006). The Federal Regulations do not stipulate what is considered an ade-quate RTI, and at present few states have done so in their state regulations. Thus, it may be that local education agencies will be required to develop these criteria for themselves. Fuchs (2003) recommends the use of a "dual discrepancy" when evaluating students' response to instruction/intervention and their need for more intensive intervention. That is to determine whether a student needs more intensive intervention (or possibly consideration for special education), the student must be discrepant from his peers in both current functioning and expected rate of growth. Further documentation of lack of progress toward age or grade-level standards can be found in classroom measures such as curriculum-embedded measures, district benchmark assessments, record review, observation, review of classroom products, and teacher and parent report.

Pattern of Strengths and Weaknesses

The second option for addressing this criterion is contained in part ii of 300.309(a)(2) and provides for the use of an alternative approach to RTI. This section states:

> "The child exhibits a pattern of strengths and weaknesses in performance, achievement, or both, relative to age, State-approved grade level standards, or intellectual development, that is determined by the group to be relevant to the identification of a specific learning disability, using appropriate assessments, consistent with §§ 300.304 and 300.305." (U.S. Department of Education, 2006, p. 46786)

This rather open alternative to an RTI approach allows teams to look at cognitive processes as well as academic performance in determining if the child may be eligible as a student with a learning disability. Indeed, though we do not advocate for it, a straightforward IQ (intellectual development) achievement discrepancy could meet this criterion. However, in addition to the numerous problems with an IQ/Achievement discrepancy approach noted by researchers (e.g., Flanagan & Ortiz, 2001; Kavale & Forness, 2000; Reynolds, 1990; Stanovich, 2005), the U.S. Department of Education argued against such an approach in its comments accompanying *IDEIA* (2004). A more reasonable interpretation of this section is to consider a pattern of strengths and weaknesses in both academic functioning and cognitive functioning that is known to be indicative of a learning disability (for this chapter, specifically dyslexia).

Berninger (1998) discusses dissociations in development as being indicative of dyslexia. These dissociations speak to the proverbial weakness in a sea of strengths and the unexpectedness of reading problems in relation to other cognitive abilities that is referred to in the International Dyslexia Association (IDA) definition of dyslexia (Lyon et al., 2003). Berninger (2007) notes that it is important to evaluate reading problems within the child's developmental context. A child who has weaknesses in all developmental areas is not likely to be showing the profile of strengths and weaknesses suggestive of dyslexia. Rather, that child's reading problems may be due to intellectual disability or pervasive developmental delay. Particularly relevant to the diagnosis of dyslexia is a student's verbal comprehension. Berninger states that a student with dyslexia should have verbal comprehension within at least the lower limits of the average range and perform on a reading or spelling measure at least one standard deviation below this score. These students would also be expected to have syntactic skills within the average range.

Flanagan, Ortiz, Alfonso, and Mascolo (2006) propose a model for the identification of learning disabilities that uses the pattern of strengths and weaknesses in performance across cognitive and academic measures to identify a student with a learning disability. Within this framework, both normative and intraindividual comparisons are made to determine the presence of relevant discrepancies and consistencies in key cognitive and academic areas. This model will be discussed more extensively later in this chapter.

Exclusionary Factors

34 CFR § 300.309(a)(3) addresses the presence of factors whose relative contributions to a student's learning problems need to be considered. This section states:

> "The group determines that its findings under paragraphs (a)(1) and (2) of this section are not primarily the result of—
>
> (i)   A visual, hearing, or motor disability;
> (ii) Mental retardation;
> (iii) Emotional disturbance;
> (iv) Cultural factors;
> (v)   Environmental or economic disadvantage; or
> (vi) Limited English proficiency." (U.S. Department of Education, 2006, pp. 46786–46787)

It is important to note that these factors may also be present for a student with a SLD, but according to the regulations they cannot be the primary cause for low achievement, failure to respond, or a pattern of strengths and weaknesses. RTI data are useful in addressing the impact of cultural and language factors when rate of progress for students who might have similar cultural or language backgrounds as the student in question is available. Both level of attainment and rate of progress toward benchmarks can be compared. Performance in academic areas not related to the area in which the student has low achievement would help document the absence of mental retardation as a primary factor. Vision, hearing, and motor screenings should be included as a matter of course in any psychoeducational evaluation. If emotional disturbance is suspected, then a screening for the presence of emotional disturbance would be important. A screening may consist of rating scales completed by the teacher and parent and/or observation of the student. If warranted, further assessment of emotional disturbance or other exclusionary factors and their contribution to low achievement would be necessary.

Appropriate Instruction

Though the aforementioned exclusionary factors are similar to previous versions of *IDEA*, the importance of access to high-quality instruction prior to consideration for special education has been elaborated on in the current regulations. An additional clause in the regulations, 34 CFR § 300.309(b) stresses the importance of appropriate instruction and documentation of progress.

> "To ensure that underachievement in a child suspected of having a specific learning disability is not due to lack of appropriate instruction in reading or math, the group must consider, as part of the evaluation described in §§ 300.304 through 300.306—
>
> (1) Data that demonstrate that prior to, or as a part of, the referral process, the child was provided appropriate instruction in regular education settings, delivered by qualified personnel; and
> (2) Data-based documentation of repeated assessments of achievement at reasonable intervals, reflecting formal assessment of student progress during instruction, which was provided to the child's parents." (U.S. Department of Education, 2006, p. 46787)

RTI processes address (b)(1) by documenting (a) the use of an appropriate research-based intervention that has been successful with other students, (b) that the intervention was implemented with fidelity, and (c) that the student was in attendance to receive the intervention. In addition, as part of an RTI process progress-monitoring data obtained from CBM, curriculum-embedded assessments, or benchmark testing will be available to address (b)(2). When such data are not available, a reporting system that is used for all children such as progress reports and grades may be sufficient to meet the need for data-based documentation.

Comprehensive Evaluation

If the conditions outlined (and illustrated in Fig. 6.1) of low achievement, lack of response to instruction or pattern of strengths and weaknesses, and consideration of exclusionary factors are met, then the "public agency must promptly request parental consent to evaluate the child to determine if the child needs special education and related services" (§ 300.309[c], p. 46787).

Since the release of the *IDEIA* (2004) regulations by the Department of Education, there has been considerable discussion around how children are identified as having a SLD. One important question has been whether lack of response to appropriate instruction is sufficient to qualify a child for services. The U.S. Department of Education's (2007) Office of Special Education Programs (OSEP) has stated the following:

1. "RTI does *not* replace a comprehensive evaluation and all other requirements required under 34 CFR §§ 300.301–300.306 (Evaluation and Reevaluations) are applicable." (slide 8)
2. "A comprehensive evaluation requires the use of a variety of data-gathering tools and strategies even if RTI is used." (slide 9)
3. "Results of RTI may be one component of the information reviewed." (slide 9)

The evaluation and re-evaluation sections referenced (34 CFR §§ 300.301–300.306) address the need to use a variety of assessment tools, assess a child in all areas of suspected disability, use technically sound, nondiscriminatory assessment procedures in an appropriate manner, and assure that the assessment is both sufficiently comprehensive to identify all of a child's special education needs and provides information directly related to the child's educational needs. 34 CFR § 300.306(b) is particularly relevant for children suspected of having dyslexia. This section reads as follows:

"Special rule for eligibility determination. A child must not be determined to be a child with a disability under this part—

(1) If the determinant factor for that determination is—
 (i) Lack of appropriate instruction in reading, including the essential components of reading instruction (as defined in section 1208(3) of the ESEA);
 (ii) Lack of appropriate instruction in math; or
 (iii) Limited English proficiency; and
(2) If the child does not otherwise meet the eligibility criteria under § 300.8(a)." (U.S. Department of Education, 2006, p. 46786)

Pertinent to this discussion of SLD and students with dyslexia is the reference to ESEA ("Elementary and Secondary Education Act"; *No Child Left Behind Act of 2001*). The section of ESEA referenced identifies the following essential components of reading instruction: phonemic awareness, phonics, vocabulary development, reading fluency, and reading comprehension strategies. Thus, as part of an evaluation, it is necessary for the team to document that the child has had reading instruction that addressed these components in a way that is "explicit and systematic" (§ 1208[3], p. 1).

Figure 6.2 provides a broad framework of assessment for a student presenting with a reading problem. As can be seen, the first step is reviewing records to determine (a) the presence of an academic deficit and (b) that the student has had research-based instruction as identified in section 300.306(b). If this condition is met, then a

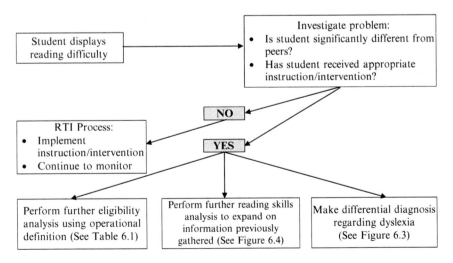

Fig. 6.2 Broad framework for reading disability assessment

comprehensive evaluation is undertaken to address the following three issues (a) eligibility analysis, (b) reading skills analysis, and (c) possible diagnosis of dyslexia.

Operational Definition of Learning Disability

One approach to eligibility analysis is the Operational Definition of LD put forth by Flanagan and colleagues (Flanagan, Ortiz, Alfonso, & Dynda, 2006; Flanagan, Ortiz, Alfonso, & Mascolo, 2002, , 2006). Table 6.1 shows how a team might proceed through an operational definition of LD for a student with reading problems. The process, as outlined in Table 6.1 (adapted from Flanagan, Ortiz, Alfonso, & Mascolo), is comprehensive and would help to address many of the eligibility criteria. It would also provide information useful to a diagnosis of dyslexia and to intervention planning.

The first step pertains to low achievement and addresses the need for the student to demonstrate a deficit in a specific academic area. Table 6.2 provides a listing of commonly used assessments that address different areas of reading. In addition to these sources of data, one might also use statewide assessments and locally normed measures. Statewide assessments provide a measure of student status in regard to grade-level state standards. With locally normed measures, the student's peers become the standard against which the child is evaluated. However, given the variation in local performance, if local data are used to determine low achievement, a nationally normed standardized test should be administered to confirm that a student is low achieving in comparison to a broader group. Informal data gathered through a structured interview with teachers and parents would also be useful in documenting underachievement. Shapiro (2004) provides guidelines for structured interviews with teachers that focus on student performance within the classroom and in comparison to peers and grade-level expectations.

At the next level, the need to assure that the deficit is not *primarily* due to factors that are included in the exclusionary criteria is addressed. Those factors include sensory impairment, cultural or linguistic differences, mental retardation, noncognitive factors, physical or health factors, and lack of instruction. Pre-referral information generated through a school-based model of tiered intervention services (such as RTI models) will be very useful in addressing this criterion. Within such a model, it is presumed that information on vision, hearing, and the impact of cultural/linguistic and other noncognitive factors will be considered as part of providing interventions. Because RTI models also emphasize appropriate interventions and monitoring of student progress, they will provide information as to the adequacy of the instruction provided.

The following step requires the administration of cognitive assessments; however, it is important to point out that the emphasis is not necessarily on generating a global IQ score. The emphasis is on the pattern of performance across cognitive tests, although a consistently low profile may suggest the need for cognitive assessment to

Table 6.1 Framework for eligibility as a student with a reading disability

Step 1	Student is referred for consideration of eligibility because of reading difficulty • Investigate previous instruction and intervention, and document within an RTI framework • Review information from teacher and parent
Step 2	Formal assessment of reading skills to determine that student is not achieving adequately for the child's age or grade-level standards • Students with learning disabilities have a significant academic deficit. Therefore, the first step in determining the presence of a reading disability that qualifies a student as needing special education services is to determine the presence of significantly discrepant reading skill • Generally, this involves performing significantly below peers or expectations for the environment • Information from multiple data sources can be useful in making the decision about the presence of an academic deficit • Standardized academic assessment in areas of concern will provide information about a deficit in relation to a larger norm group • Also, review performance in other academic areas with record review or brief academic screener
Step 3	Determine if the reading deficit is due *primarily* to one of the exclusionary factors • This step requires sufficient assessment or record review to determine whether the reading problem is due primarily to • Cultural-linguistic issues • Noncognitive factors such as motivation, emotional disturbance • Mental retardation • Sensory impairment or health • Insufficient instruction
Step 4	Cognitive assessment to evaluate appropriate areas of development and rule out other disabling conditions • Though you may not need a global IQ score, you need sufficient information to determine that the student does not have a more pervasive delay that is the primary cause of the reading problem • It is important to determine that there is an area of cognitive weakness both relative to the general population (normative difference) and relative to the student's overall cognitive profile • For a reading disability, it will be important to evaluate cognitive processes linked to reading: phonological processing, rapid naming, working memory, language • When a particular cognitive deficit is identified, it is important to revisit the exclusionary criteria to make sure that the deficit is not due to any of these criteria
Step 5	Analysis of cognitive academic profile • The analysis of the cognitive/academic profile serves to determine if the pattern of strengths and weaknesses is consistent with a reading disability • A student with dyslexia will demonstrate cognitive processing weaknesses in those areas related to reading, but will not show an overall language delay
Step 6	Determination that the reading disability is affecting the student's performance to a significant degree and the student's needs cannot be met without special education • The purpose of this final step is to assure that the impact of reading disability is of such magnitude that the student needs special education in accordance with *IDEIA* (2004)

Adapted from Flanagan, Ortiz, Alfonso, and Mascolo (2006)

Table 6.2 Commonly used reading assessments

	Phon. aware	Phonics	Fluency	Rapid naming	Reading Comp.	Oral lang.	Other
Reading-specific tests							
Comprehensive test of phonological awareness	√			√			PM
Test of word reading efficiency			√				
Gray oral reading test			√		√		
Gray silent reading test					√		
Process assessment of the learner II	√	√	√	√	√		MP OP
Comprehensive achievement batteries							
Kaufman Test of Educational Achievement II	√	√	√	√	√	√	
Woodcock Johnson Tests of Achievement III		√	√	√	√	√	
Wechsler Individual Achievement Test		√			√	√	

PM phonological memory, *MP* morphological processing, *OP* orthographic processing

aid in the possible diagnosis of mental retardation. The purpose of this step is to determine whether there is a weakness in any specific area of cognitive processing and if that area is associated with reading. In other words, this step in the operational definition addresses the deficit in a basic psychological process that is part of the definition of SLD and goes further in seeking to determine whether the area of cognitive weakness may be causally related to the area of academic weakness. Likewise, it would be expected that the student does not show deficits in areas of cognitive functioning that are not related to the area of low achievement. Table 6.3 lists the cognitive processes considered to be linked to reading disabilities. As can be seen in this table, a weakness in phonological processing would be associated with reading difficulties, whereas a weakness in spatial reasoning is not typically related to reading problems.

As part of this level, the exclusionary factors are again reviewed to assure that the cognitive deficits are not due to any of these factors. To proceed to the next step, two criteria must have been met at this level (a) identification of a normative deficit in at least one area of cognitive ability/processing and (b) identification of an empirical or logical link between low functioning in an identified area of cognitive ability/process-ing and a corresponding weakness in academic performance (Flanagan, Ortiz, Alfonso, & Mascolo, 2006, p. 820).

The next step is to determine if the aptitude/achievement pattern is consistent with a definition of LD. This is not the same as the traditional IQ/achievement discrepancy. The purpose is not to look at one full scale score; rather the purpose is to evaluate the overall performance on cognitive and achievement tests seeking to determine if there is specificity in the learning difficulty. The following are important points to consider at this level:

- The student has deficits in both academic and cognitive areas and these deficits are related to each other.

Table 6.3 Cognitive processes associated with reading achievement

Stronger association with reading achievement
• Language development, lexical knowledge, and listening ability at all ages
• Phonological awareness/processing during early elementary years
• Rapid naming during early elementary years
• Perceptual speed during all school years, but particularly elementary years

Weaker association with reading achievement
• Inductive and general sequential reasoning related to reading comprehension
• Memory span particularly in relation to working memory
• Orthographic processing

Adapted from Flanagan, Ortiz, Alfonso, and Mascolo 2006

- The student demonstrates a pattern of normal functioning outside these areas of deficit. Students with learning disabilities exhibit deficits in specific areas. A student with low functioning across all areas may need further evaluation for mild mental retardation.
- It has been demonstrated that the academic and cognitive deficits are not due to any exclusionary factors.

Given that these criteria are met, the final step requires a decision as to the "substantial impact" of the learning disability. This criterion acts as a safety net for determining the "need for special education" as identified in *IDEIA* (2004) as one purpose of the comprehensive evaluation. It is possible (though unlikely) that a student may have a learning disability as identified through this operational definition, but still be functioning adequately within the classroom. In such an instance, the child would not meet criteria for special education services.

Diagnosis of Dyslexia

While the operational definition described will lead to eligibility determination and provide useful information as to a child's strengths and weaknesses in critical cognitive and academic areas, further assessment may be needed to fully understand and plan for the educational needs of a child with dyslexia. In addition, there is a wide body of research (Adams, 1990; Berninger et al., 2006; Berninger & Richards, 2002; Richards et al., 2006; Shaywitz, 2003; Torgesen, 2002a, 2002b; Vellutino, Tunmer, Jaccard, & Chen, 2007) supporting the notion that there are significant *components* that contribute to the reading process and that if these are known and when relevant intervened upon, interventions are more powerful. However, there are some who do not necessarily dispute this, but tend to see these multiple components as perhaps not as useful as simple reading measures (Hammill, 2004; Swanson, Trainin, Necoechea, & Hammill, 2003). So in terms of assessing for dyslexia, when and how should it be done?

We align ourselves with the more neuropsychologically oriented approach believing that when we know more about the student in terms of helping to think through how to intervene, ultimately the better that will be for the student. However, there is always the real-world aspect of how long does it take and therefore how much would it cost. It is hoped that within a school using a multi-tiered approach to providing early reading interventions (such as RTI) fewer students would require comprehensive evaluations as early and appropriate instruction and intervention would have remediated their reading problems (Hale & Fiorello, 2004). It is those students whose reading problems are not due to instructional deficits who are then referred for a comprehensive evaluation that will inform eligibility decisions, instructional planning, and the diagnosis of dyslexia.

Berninger (2007) suggests that the following domains should be assessed (a) cognition and memory, (b) receptive and expressive language, (c) gross and fine motor, (d) attention and executive functioning, and (e) social-emotional functioning when evaluating a student who appears to have a reading disability. The evaluation of each of these domains will serve to allow for differential diagnosis of dyslexia as the cause of a student's reading problems as opposed to other disorders such as AD/HD or oral language delays. This information is important as interventions that are effective with a group of children not displaying AD/HD or oral language delays, for example, may not be effective with those who do. Thus, the differential diagnosis provided by a comprehensive approach to assessment will inform instructional planning. In addition to these domains for assessment, Berninger also recommends assessing morphological, orthographic, and syntactical awareness as well as phonological awareness to further differentiate between students with dyslexia and those with oral and written language disorder. Berninger provides check sheets and flow charts in the *Process Assessment of the Learner* (2nd ed.; PAL II) that guide the user through the diagnostic process.

The definition of dyslexia adopted by the International Dyslexia Association (Lyon et al., 2003) and presented in Chap. 1 also provides useful guidelines for making a diagnosis of dyslexia. The first component to consider is the following "It is characterized by difficulties with accurate and/or fluent word recognition and by poor spelling and decoding abilities" (p. 2). A diagnosis of dyslexia requires that a student demonstrate deficits in basic word-level skills. The deficits may be evidenced through reading or spelling difficulties and may or may not involve either rate or accuracy. Thus, a student who is an accurate decoder, but extremely slow, may have dyslexia. Therefore, a diagnosis of dyslexia requires careful analysis of a student's reading skills.

The definition further notes that problems in reading comprehension or vocabulary are secondary to the word-level deficits. Thus, a child who has only deficits in comprehension, though the student may exhibit difficulties in reading, would not likely be considered to have dyslexia. Indeed, most children with dyslexia will perform better on reading comprehension tasks than they do on basic reading tasks such as decoding.

One must also determine that the difficulties are "unexpected in relation to other cognitive abilities and the provision of appropriate instruction" (Lyon et al., 2003, p. 2). Reviewing data generated within an RTI approach and steps 1, 2, 3, and 4 of the operational definition described will provide information useful in addressing this element of the definition. It will eliminate lack of instruction and other developmental disorders as a cause of the reading problem. The assessment of cognitive abilities and analysis of the pattern of strengths and weaknesses discussed in step 5 of the operational definition will address the issue of unexpectedness. A student with dyslexia will demonstrate verbal skills and general ability at the average range or better while displaying weaknesses in areas related to dyslexia and discussed later.

The definition broadly states that the difficulties "typically result from a deficit in the phonological component of language" (Lyon et al., 2003, p. 2). The phonological component of language is measured through tests of phonological processing and phonological memory. Naming speed is considered by some to be a phonological component of language though we have presented the position of Maryanne Wolf and others (Bowers & Wolf, 1993; Bowers, Sunseth, & Golden, 1999; Wolf & Bowers, 1999) that naming speed represents a separate cognitive process. It seems to us that there is sufficient evidence to warrant considering a deficit in naming speed as a possible marker for dyslexia independent of more frequently noted phonological deficits. As discussed in the operational definition, the student should perform at a level significantly discrepant (about 1 standard deviation) from the child's peers and own overall functioning in one of these areas.

Finally, dyslexia is defined as "neurobiological in origin" meaning that the student has a processing deficit that has been identified as linked to dyslexia (Lyon et al., 2003, p. 2). The student's performance on a measure of rapid naming, phonological processing, or orthographic processing should be below the average range and low in comparison to the child's score on other cognitive processing measures.

In summary, when diagnosing a student with dyslexia, the practitioner should be able to answer "yes" to the following:

- Does the student perform significantly below his or her peers on a measure of basic literacy such as word reading or decoding?
- Has the student had sufficient instruction?
- Have you determined that the difficulties identified earlier are not due to another factor such as mental retardation, AD/HD, or emotional disturbance?
- Does the student have a deficit in phonological processing, orthographic processing, and/or rapid naming?
- Does the student have oral language abilities within the average range?

If the team can answer "yes" to all of the above, then a diagnosis of dyslexia should be considered. Figure 6.3 provides a worksheet to use in considering this diagnosis.

English Learners

Assessing students for whom English is their second language presents unique challenges. If a child's reading problems are due to language or cultural factors, then they are not considered to be a child with a disability. When evaluating an

Dyslexia Assessment Worksheet

Name _____ Birth date _____Grade_____

Teacher _____ School _____

Parent(s)_____

Evidence of academic deficit		
Student performs below the average range in basic reading skill. Among older students the academic deficit may be primarily in spelling and reading fluency.		
Test	**Standard Score**	**Percentile Rank**

The academic deficit is not due to lack of instruction
Describe previous instruction and interventions and outcomes. Attach completed intervention worksheets for tier 1 and/or tier 2 (see attached).

The academic deficit is not due to other developmental causes or to language/cultural factors.
Provide data regarding rating scales, cognitive assessments, and observations to address the following.

Factor	Evidence
Sensory impairment	
Mental retardation	
Emotional disturbance	
Cultural factors	
Environmental disadvantage	
Limited English proficiency	
Other neurological or genetic disorder	

Cognitive processing deficit related to reading.
The student shows a significant weakness in one of the following areas: phonological processing, rapid naming,and/or orthographic processing.

Fig. 6.3 A worksheet to use in considering diagnosis of dyslexia

English Learner for dyslexia, best practice requires assessment in both languages (Tabors & Snow, 2002). Geva (2000) suggests that measuring phonological processing and comparing oral language and written language proficiency are useful in identifying English Learners with reading disability. She reports that such

Test	Standard Score	Percentile Rank

Oral language skills in average range
Provide a measure(s) of verbal comprehension that is within the average range.

Test	Standard Score	Percentile Rank

Verbal comprehension is significantly better than reading skills
Provide comparison of measures that demonstrate significant difference between performance on oral language skills and reading skill (either basic reading, comprehension, or possibly spelling)

Verbal comprehension measure(s):		
Reading skills measure(s):		

Explanation of difference using approximately one standard deviation or confidence intervals

Summary statement on dyslexia
Provide a summary statement as to the diagnosis of dyslexia based on the above information and other pertinent information.

Fig. 6.3 (continued)

methods can be used prior to a child's achieving competency in the second language. In their practice guide on effective literacy and English language instruction for English learners, Gersten et al. (2007) conclude that oral language proficiency is a poor predictor of basic reading achievement for young English learners. Geva also recommends looking at the trajectory of growth in both phonological processing and basic reading skills. Comparing a given child to the rate of others can provide information regarding a reading disability. Geva and Yaghoube-Zadeh (2006) found that among a variety of measures phonological awareness, rapid letter naming and word recognition were the strongest predictors of reading competence among second-grade readers. The Web site http://www.colorincolorado.org provides useful information to parents and teachers on the reading development of English Learners.

Intervention Worksheet: Results of Tier 1 - 2 (circle one)

Student _____	Grade _____
Teacher _____	Room _____

Name of intervention: _____

_____ Linked to curriculum?

_____ Research based (source of information)? _____

_____ Small group (# of students in the group)? _____

_____ Individualized?

_____ Computer based?

Minutes per session?   _____

Number of sessions per week?   _____

Total # of sessions for this student?   _____

Total # of sessions offered to this student?   _____

Progress monitoring   :

Goal   _____ correct words read per minute

Level at referral   _____

Current baseline   _____

How often?   _____ per week

Level of median student if available   _____

Relevant benchmarks _____

_____

Progress of other students if available:

Attach any progress monitoring graphs

Any changes in intervention made in response to data?

_____

_____

Fig. 6.3 (continued)

Flanagan, Ortiz, and Alfonso (2007) also provide guidelines for the assessment of bilingual children suspected of having learning disabilities. The framework rests in an analysis of subtests as to their language and cultural loading and comparing student performance across these subtests. The reader is referred to this reference book for further information.

Reading Skills Analysis

As part of any assessment of reading, it is important to provide information that identifies gaps in critical skills. The rubric outlined in Fig. 6.4 provides a flow chart for an intervention-focused assessment of a student with reading problems. This chart is not necessarily meant to represent the order in which assessments would be done. Rather it flows from the more global processes (i.e., reading comprehension) down to the more specific (e.g., phonological processing). Within any assessment of reading disability, one should assure that each of these areas has been assessed.

Reading Fluency

Problems in reading comprehension may stem from difficulties with fluent reading. This would be an initial analysis of reading skill. Both oral and silent reading fluency can be evaluated. Measures of oral reading fluency include *Gray Oral Reading Test* (4th ed.; GORT; Wiederhold & Bryant, 2001); curriculum-based measures (CBM; e.g., DIBELS, Good et al., 2003; available http://dibels.uoregon.edu); *Gray Test of Silent Reading* (GTSR; Wiederhold & Blalock, 2000); and the *Woodcock Johnson Tests of Achievement* (3rd ed., WJ III; Woodcock, McGrew, & Mather, 2001).

Oral Language

If a student's fluency rate is adequate, then a problem in reading comprehension may be due to more pervasive language difficulties. Thus, it is important to evaluate receptive oral language. A student whose reading problems are due to deficits in language

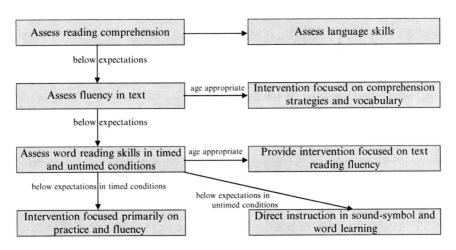

Fig. 6.4 Skills-based reading assessment

comprehension does not have dyslexia. Rather the child needs interventions focused on language development. In fact, a hallmark of dyslexia is better oral language comprehension than text comprehension. It is unlikely that any student who did not have severe auditory processing or hearing impairment would read at a significantly greater level than performing on oral language comprehension tests. There are numerous assessments of oral language, many of which are administered by speech and language therapists. Three of the more common instruments that may be used to assess a student's oral language comprehension include the *Test* of *Language Development-Primary* (3rd ed.; TOLD-P:3; Newcomber & Hammill, 1997), the *Test of Language Development-Intermediate* (3rd ed.; TOLD-I:3; Hammill & Newcomber, 1997), and the *Clinical Evaluation of Language Function* (4th ed. CELF-4; Semel, Wiig, & Secord, 2003). Vocabulary measures are also used to evaluate language skills. Comprehensive assessment batteries incorporate evaluation of oral language comprehension along with other academic measures. These are useful in that one can compare scores on reading comprehension to oral language comprehension within the same test battery, thus eliminating norm group differences. These include the WJ III (Woodcock et al., 2001) and the Kaufman Test of Educational Achievement (2nd ed.; KTEA-II; Kaufman & Kaufman, 2004).

Word Reading

If a student has poor oral reading fluency, then the examiner should evaluate the student's word reading skills. For students who read accurately but slowly in either text or on word lists, the intervention will likely begin with a focus on increasing fluency. However, if accuracy is poor then these skills must also be addressed. Evaluation of a student's word reading skills requires assessing both accuracy and fluency with both real and nonsense words in timed and untimed situations. Table 6.4 provides a matrix identifying the components and processes of word-level assessment. Table 6.5 provides examples of tests assessing each of these components. Untimed tests of nonsense and real word reading provide information as to whether the student has requisite word reading accuracy. Untimed tests of nonword or nonsense word reading assess decoding knowledge: how much information the student has about the letter sound correspondences of English (phonics). There are

Table 6.4 Word-level processes assessed

	Real words	Nonsense word
Decoding		
Timed	Automaticity of word retrieval	Automaticity of decoding
Untimed	Lexicon	Phonics knowledge
Encoding		
Timed		
Untimed	Orthographic knowledge Lexicon	Phonics knowledge

Table 6.5 Tests of word-level processes

	Real words	Nonsense word
Decoding		
Timed	TOWRE	TOWRE
	KTEA II	KTEA II
Untimed	KTEA II	KTEA II
	WJ III	WJ III
	Most achievement batteries	Most achievement batteries
Encoding		
Timed	CBM Word List	
Untimed	KTEA II	Spelling of Sounds on WJ III
	WJ III	
	Spelling tests	

numerous tests of phonics or decoding knowledge. Most achievement batteries, such as the WJ III (Woodcock et al., 2001) and the KTEA II (Kaufman & Kaufman, 2004), include them. They are also available on reading tests such as (and see Table 6.2) the *Woodcock-Johnson Diagnostic Reading Battery* (WJ DRB; Woodcock et al.) and the *Process Assessment of the Learner* (2nd ed.; PAL II; Berninger, 2007).

Lists of real words, because they contain words that cannot be read correctly through decoding strategies alone, provide an assessment of the student's lexicon or mental storehouse of words. The achievement batteries listed here contain tests of real word reading as well as nonsense word reading. The results of these tests also can be helpful as assessments of a student's morphological knowledge. The PAL II (Berninger, 2007) is the only test battery that provides explicit tests of morphological knowledge.

Timed tests of real and nonsense word reading provide information as to whether the student has fluency in word identification. Until the publication of the *Test of Word Reading Efficiency* (TOWRE; Torgesen, Wagner, & Rashotte, 1999) such measures were not available, though there were tests of reading fluency for connected text. Currently available tests of timed reading of both real and nonsense words include the TOWRE, the KTEA II (Kaufman & Kaufman, 2002), and the PAL II (Berninger, 2007). The TOWRE and the KTEA II provide word lists as stimuli. The TOWRE only provides speeded measures, whereas the KTEA II provides untimed measures for comparison. The PAL II takes a more comprehensive approach to assessing word fluency. It includes a decoding fluency task similar to that of the TOWRE and the KTEA II. However, it includes two different tasks measuring real word reading. The first, Morphological Decoding Fluency, requires the reading of words that have the same base but different suffixes. The second, Word Choice Fluency, requires the examinee to identify the correctly spelled version among an array of phonologically accurate misspellings. These two tests also have an option for scoring of accuracy as well as fluency.

Curriculum-based measures such as the DIBELS (Good et al., 2003) or *AIMSWeb Early Literacy Skills* also provide fluency measures for real and nonsense word reading. These measures have multiple forms and can be used for repeated assessments as part of progress monitoring for a student receiving interventions. Analysis of these measures can also provide information about a student's understanding and mastery of basic reading skills. *I've DIBEL'd, Now What?* (Hall, 2006) offers guidelines for instructional grouping based on student performance on DIBELS or similar early literacy fluency measures.

Comparing a student's scores in timed and untimed situations and with real and nonsense words provides information useful to intervention planning. A student who is accurate, but lacks fluency in word reading for both real and nonsense words may not need further instruction in phonics. Rather the child may need an intervention focused on increasing mastery and fluency. A student who is accurate at reading nonsense words, but inaccurate at reading real words is failing to develop a lexicon of "sight" words. This student's intervention may need to focus more on word recognition than on learning to decode. The student who is accurate with real words, but has trouble with nonsense words may need instruction in decoding.

Spelling Tests

In addition to information gleaned from tests of decoding print to sound (reading), encoding or spelling tests can provide valuable information regarding a student's developing knowledge of the English language and its alphabet. Spelling tests can provide information about a student's understanding of and ability to apply phonics to the spelling of words and of a student's orthographic and morphological awareness. Traditional spelling tests can be examined to determine whether a student uses "legal" or "illegal" letter combinations and whether the child's spellings reflect knowledge of conventions such as *le* endings. For example the student who spells "tell" as "tle" is beginning to notice graphemic conventions. The student who puts odd letter combinations together such as "kpz" does not have a good sense of English orthography. Spellings also provide information about a student's morphological awareness. For example, the student who spells "lived" as "livt" does not have knowledge of the "ed" convention for past tense. Most achievement tests contain these traditional spelling tests.

Tests that ask students to spell nonsense words are less common but are useful in assessing a student's knowledge of phonics. The WJ III Spelling of Sounds subtest is one such test. Of course, student response to traditional spelling tests will also provide information about their phonics knowledge. Words that are spelled incorrectly, but phonetically suggest that the student is developing mastery of phonics, but not creating accessible word representations in his or her mental lexicon.

Virginia Berninger (2007), author of the PAL II, provides the most refined measures of a student's knowledge about the English language print-sound system. The subtests of the PAL II provide measures of a student's orthographic, morphological, and phonological knowledge. Orthographic knowledge is measured with tasks that require the student to quickly code and recall letters within words, and to identify words spelled correctly among an array of phonetically correct words. Morphological knowledge is assessed through tasks measuring a student's understanding of prefixes and suffixes.

Assessment of Cognitive Processes

For students who do not seem to be developing basic reading skills, further evaluation of related cognitive processes is important. Those processes include phonological awareness, naming speed, phonological memory, and language. There are numerous tests providing these measures. If the framework for determining eligibility outlined in the operational definition of LD and the areas of differential diagnosis identified by Berninger (2007) have been evaluated, this information will already be available. However, it may be appropriate to assess these processes for some students prior to consideration for special education and a comprehensive evaluation. For a student who is not responding to an early level intervention provided either in the classroom or through supplemental support (e.g., Tier 1 or Tier 2), knowing whether the student had weakness in a cognitive process important to reading development could be helpful to intervention design (Berninger; Feifer & DeFina, 2000; Hale & Fiorello, 2004).

Phonological awareness is assessed through tasks that require the student to manipulate the sounds in words. Examples of such tests include clusters on the WJ III (Woodcock et al., 2007), the KTEA II (Kaufman & Kaufman, 2002), the PAL II (Berninger, 2007), and the *Comprehensive Test of Phonological Processing* (CTOPP; Wagner, Torgesen, & Rashotte, 1999). Naming speed is evaluated through tests that require the student to name as fast as possible letters, numbers, colors, or objects. Naming speed subtests are also available on the noted tests. Verbal memory is assessed through rote memory tasks that require the memorization of number strings, letter/number strings, words, sentences, and/or stories. The PAL II among others provides a test of verbal working memory. The CTOPP provides a test of phonological memory that requires the student to repeat back nonsense words, thus negating meaning-related memory supports.

If a student, who is in a Tier 1 intervention (within an RTI model), displays deficits in key areas such as phonological awareness or naming speed, and has a family history of reading problems, this may indicate a need to intervene more intently or to monitor progress more closely than might be the case for a child who does not show such underlying cognitive deficits.

Age at Identification

Though dyslexia is defined as problems at the word level and is associated with difficulties in basic literacy skills of decoding and word recognition, there are some children who will compensate sufficiently to develop basic reading skills. For example, problems in phonological processing may be compensated for through strong syntactic or semantic skills (Snowling, 2005). However, often these children will exhibit lingering literacy-related deficits as they encounter more difficult and lengthy text and in writing. Indeed, dyslexia-related symptoms can impact them into adulthood (Goldberg, Higgins, Raskin, & Herman, 2003). Therefore, it would not be appropriate to assume that if a child has not exhibited reading problems until middle childhood,

Table 6.6 Typical reading demands and profile of older dyslexic student

Need for oral language proficiency increases ↑	Need for word specific knowledge increases ↓	Oral comprehension	stronger than	Reading comprehension
		Reading comprehension	stronger than	Word reading accuracy
		Real word reading	stronger than	Nonsense word reading

the student does not have dyslexia. Children with dyslexia who do not come to the attention of school psychologists or other specialists until later elementary or early middle school years may demonstrate problems in the following areas:

- Slower-than-expected reading speed
- Poor spelling
- Poor handwriting
- Problems with new more technical vocabulary
- Problems with foreign languages

Table 6.6 provides the characteristics of the typical profile of an older student with dyslexia. A careful analysis of their reading skills (as described earlier) will often reveal unequal development across skill areas. For example, a student with strong oral language skills, but weak decoding skills, will often perform as shown in Fig. 6.4. This figure indicates that as a literacy-related task relies more on basic reading skills and can be less supported by language comprehension, the student will do relatively less well. When confronted with such a student, a careful review of the child's educational history may reveal early problems in reading development.

Concluding Comments

The psychoeducational assessment of a student with reading problems must address these questions (a) Does the child qualify for and need special education services? and (b) What interventions will best meet this student's needs? Though these two questions are the most critical in a school setting determining whether the reading problem is due to dyslexia is also important. Such a differential diagnosis is helpful to school staff, parents, and ultimately the student in understanding the student's learning strengths and weakness, knowing what to expect in the future, and educational planning.

Chapter 7
Treatment

Reading is a complex neurobiological process that we are just beginning to understand. Because dyslexia is most often considered to be an academic problem, school-based practitioners need tools to better diagnose the disorder (as discussed in Chap. 6) and strategies to better intervene. In particular, since the passage of PL 94-142, or the Education for All Handicapped Children Act of 1975, it is clear that interventions have to be provided to students identified with a specific learning disability (SLD). Dyslexia is currently included in the most recent reauthorization of PL 94-142, the *Individuals with Disabilities Education Act,* (IDEA), as a diagnosis that "fits" under SLD. However, as with previous versions of this law, *IDEIA* does not specify how dyslexia is defined or how it is to be treated. Nevertheless, it is clear that as many as 80% of the students served in the SLD category have reading problems (Lyon et al., 2001). For this reason,, it is incumbent upon school-based personnel and school psychologists to be aware of how to treat this developmental disorder and to be able to help construct an Individual Educational Plan (IEP) to better ensure the success of these children.

Although over the last 30 years the growth in intervention research has followed the burst in knowledge about dyslexia, much more research is needed. We have a clearer understanding of what sorts of treatments work for some of the symptoms of dyslexia, but do not have good evidence-based, highly effective interventions, for all symptoms. This chapter reviews a few important guidelines for choosing which reading interventions to try when helping a student with dyslexia. To accomplish this, we will first review the National Reading Panel's suggestions of the types of interventions it recommends; then review the International Dyslexia Association's (IDA) suggestions for interventions needed for children experiencing dyslexia; and finally review some of what are frequently referred to as core reading programs, comprehensive reading programs, and supplemental intervention reading programs. Those programs that have some research base are presented. Since the National Reading Panel (2000) report was published, a number of programs have been developed citing that they have an *evidence base*, but in fact they have no *research base*. Rather, many of these programs are developed from the recommendations made in the National Reading Panel Report and have not themselves been empirically validated. The final section focuses on what are considered by

C. Christo et al., *Identifying, Assessing, and Treating Dyslexia at School*,
DOI: 10.1007/978-0-387-88600-8_7, © Springer Science + Business Media, LLC 2009

most to be *controversial therapies*, or those that are currently considered by most to be nonstandard alternatives to the treatment of dyslexia.

National Reading Panel's Report and Recommendations

The National Institute for Child Health and Human Development along with the Department of Education convened the National Reading Panel (2000) to provide a meta-analysis of the reading research in the areas of alphabetics, comprehension, fluency, teacher education, and technology from 1966 to 1997. A methodology committee set the criteria for those studies that would be included. Due to the rigor of the criteria and sometimes to the number of actual studies available, only the area of alphabetics was analyzed via the use of meta-analytic techniques. However, literature reviews and at least partial conclusions were drawn where possible regarding the other areas.

The meta-analytic findings in the area of *alphabetics* suggest that direct instruction in phonemic awareness when coupled with systematic phonics instruction yielded very statistically significant results with gains that were maintained over time. This is probably one of the most well-documented "facts" in neuroscience and education and is considered by the authors to be a truly impressive finding (National Reading Panel, 2000).

In the area of *fluency*, the panel decided to examine studies of guided oral reading and independent silent reading, rather than research on more specific fluency training programs or strategies. Neither guided reading nor independent silent reading was found to be particularly powerful, with the panel concluding that more methodologically rigorous research needs to be designed and implemented. However, the practitioner's dilemma is that fluency very clearly is not increased if there is *no* direct explicit instruction, and there is a beginning body of evidence that if decoding is overemphasized at the expense of fluency, fluency can be negatively impacted (National Reading Panel, 2000).

In the *comprehension* area, the panel noted three predominant themes in the research: vocabulary instruction, text comprehension instruction, and teacher preparation and comprehension strategies instruction. Again, there was no formal meta-analysis done in any of these areas although the panel did suggest that vocabulary instruction leads to gains in comprehension. In addition, it was noted that findings suggested certain teacher strategies are useful. More specifically they stated that:

> "First, vocabulary should be taught both directly and indirectly. Repetition and multiple exposures to vocabulary items are important. Learning in rich contexts, incidental learning, and use of computer technology all enhance the acquisition of vocabulary. Direct instruction should include restructuring as necessary and should actively engage the student. Finally, dependence on a single vocabulary instruction method will not result in optimal learning." (National Reading Panel, 2000, p. 14)

In *text comprehension instruction*, the findings again suggested that teaching a combination of comprehension strategies is most effective, although teaching teachers how to make this happen is under-researched. Panel members identified 16 categories of text comprehension from which they concluded that the following seven have a fairly good research base:

1. "*Comprehension monitoring* – where readers learn how to be aware of their understanding of the material;
2. *Cooperative learning* – where students learn reading strategies together;
3. *Use of graphic and semantic organizers* (including story maps) – where readers make graphic representations of the material to assist comprehension;
4. *Question answering* – where readers answer question posed by the teacher and receive immediate feedback;
5. *Question generation* – where readers ask themselves questions about various aspects of the story;
6. *Story structure* – where students are taught to use the structure of the story as a means of helping them recall story content in order to answer questions about what they have read; and
7. *Summarization* – where readers are taught to integrate ideas and generalize form the text information." (p. 15)

In the third area, the panel noted that the studies they found could be incorporated into two predominant approaches: direct instruction and transactional strategy instruction. The *direct instruction* approach is simply where the teacher very explicitly reviews the reasoning and/or thinking processes involved in reading comprehension. Thus, they teach students to view comprehension as a problem-solving task and to think strategically about solving comprehension problems. *Transactional strategy instruction* also includes explicit instruction of problem solving, but can also emphasize the facilitation of student discussions via a collaboration model to aid deeper understandings. The main finding of the panel was that a great deal more research is needed and that extensive formal instruction in reading comprehension *for teachers* is needed (National Reading Panel, 2000).

In the fourth area, *teacher education and reading instruction*, the panel tried to find research on both preservice and in-service instruction. The panel's findings emphasized that more research was needed, especially for preservice instruction. They did note that the research generally supported that in-service training led to significantly higher student achievement and showed positive effects on teaching (National Reading Panel, 2000).

Finally, in the area of *computer technology and reading instruction*, contemporary technologies are providing new and rich research areas. However, because it is so new, few studies met the panel's criteria for inclusion. As will be discussed later in this chapter, more data have become available since the panel's report. The panel's conclusions at the time of the report were that, with the addition of speech to computer presented text, computer technology could be used for reading instruction. The panel also noted that hypertext for support and word processing to better integrate reading and writing skill development are promising areas of intervention (National Reading Panel, 2000).

International Dyslexia Association Recommendations

Although the IDA previously known as the Orton Society does not formally endorse
any one intervention program over another, historically, the Fernald Method (Fernald
& Keller, 1921), or what later became referred to as the VAKT approach (visual,
auditory, kinesthetic, and tactile), did become the major intervention approach of its
time for dyslexia. This was to a significant extent due to the fact that it was the first
innovative intervention postulated to be effective for learning disabled students.
While it did not prove to be a fruitful approach to treating dyslexia, it did move the
field toward VAKT strategies as approaches to treating dyslexia. One of the major
problems at that time was that research had not yet revealed the core symptoms of
dyslexia. More recently, useful aspects of the Fernald Method have been incorporated within the Orton–Gillingham approach (Gillingham & Stillman, 1960, 1970).
This approach, which became the staple for treatment since its inception, evolved
into a variety of other intervention models (see later). It was developed by Gillingham
and Stillman as a tutorial model for one-to-one instruction for dyslexic children and
adults. June Orton (1976) described the basic tenets of the Orton–Gillingham
approach as:

1. "It is a direct instruction approach to the study of synthetic phonics presenting
   the sounds of the phonograms orally as separate units and then teaching the
   process of blending them into syllables and words.
2. It is an integrated, multisensory approach. Each unit and sequence is established
   through hearing, speaking, seeing, and writing. Auditory, visual, and kinesthetic
   patterns reinforce each other, a feature that also provides for individual needs
   among the students.
3. It is a systematic, step-by-step approach, proceeding from the simpler to the more
   complex in orderly progression in an upward spiral of language development."
   (p. 11)

Most recently, this "multisensory" approach to instruction has become known as
"Multisensory Structured Language Education" (MSLE; Wilson & Schupack,
1997). Both the Orton–Gillingham and the MSLE have developed organizations for
training teachers in their respective intervention programs.

The core features of MSLE take a great deal from its predecessors. As Berninger
(Berninger & Richards, 2002) and others have pointed out, reading is a relatively new
skill on the evolutionary ladder. Given this fact, humans are not yet "hard wired" for
it, as we are for language acquisition. Multiple neurological systems must interact to
develop a working neural network for efficient reading. A useful metaphor for what
happens to students with dyslexia is that they do not "intuitively" learn the rules and/
or code required for reading, spelling, and writing. However, they can learn, but will
need explicit teaching with a well-structured and sequenced curriculum.

The MSLE group believes that this style of curriculum also needs to be taught in
a particular way, and that is from a multimodal or multisensory framework. Perhaps
the biggest difference between the MSLE and Orton–Gillingham approaches is that
the MSLE stresses that both analytic (whole-to-part) and synthetic (part-to-whole)

instruction in phonemic awareness and decoding needs to take place and that reading, spelling, and writing must be part of an integrated curriculum of instruction. The Orton–Gillingham approach favors utilizing the blending or synthetic approach and does not necessarily endorse the more comprehensive approach.

More specifically, the Education Task Force of IDA has proposed specific criteria that they believe are necessary for teaching students with dyslexia and they stress that both content and process are important. The MSLE group has responded to this and adopted the IDA principles. In terms of content, programs must contain instruction in phonological awareness (the smallest unit of sound that can be distinguished as a distinct sound belonging to a particular language), alphabetics (phoneme/grapheme, or sound/symbol, correspondence), syllable instruction/morphology (smallest unit of meaning within a language), syntax (the principles that dictate the sequence and function of words in an order that conveys meaning), and semantics/comprehension (the aspect of language concerned with meaning). The process recommended consists of continuing to use VAKT to teach all skills to aid attention and encoding, and continuing to use direct instruction rather than any more inferential strategies. In addition, they believe that this approach helps to ensure that the student will master the material that is presented in a systematic and cumulative fashion, that the teachers are trained well enough to utilize the diagnostic teaching necessary to monitor and change strategies as needed, and, as referred to earlier, that instruction encompass both analytic and synthetic strategies when addressing any of the content areas.

Programs, Curricula, and Interventions: Prevention and Intervention

Programs are those vehicles that require a school to promote wide-ranging changes to its curriculum and have prevention as their primary target. Curricula will be those programs that can be purchased by a school or a district to be the primary or basal reading programs for the school and tend to be prevention focused, but in different formats can sometimes be used for Tier 1 and perhaps even Tier 2 interventions. They frequently have a scope and sequence of instruction for children with potential language-based difficulties. Intervention-oriented programs are used sometimes for Tier 2, but primarily for Tier 3 interventions and are focused on children that are diagnosed with or believed to have dyslexia and are usually delivered in one-to-one or very small group format and in a time- and labor-intensive fashion.

Programs

Perhaps the two programs that best capture the spirit of changing multiple aspects of school functioning to promote reading excellence are *Success for All* (SFA; Slavin & Madden, 1999; Slavin, Madden, Karweit, Dolan, & Wasik, 1992) and

Direct Instructional System of Teaching Arithmetic and Reading (DISTAR; Becker, 1977; Engelmann & Bruner, 1983).

SFA began its development in 1986 at the request of Baltimore's school superintendent and taken on by Slavin and his colleagues at the Johns Hopkins Center for Research on the Education of Students Placed at Risk. Their goal was to re-create how an elementary school should function to maximize the likelihood of educational excellence for its students. With that in mind, they constructed a system of organization and instruction that was piloted in the Baltimore school system. They developed a comprehensive reading curriculum, *Reading Roots* and *Reading Wings* (Madden, 1995; Madden et al., 1996). *Reading Roots* was developed for the K to first graders and *Reading Wings* was developed for the second to fifth graders. Although these curricula do not meet MSLE criteria, the curricula are engaging and do cover most of the areas suggested by that group, especially language development, phonemic awareness, alphabetics, and phonics. Reading is also integrated with written expression (Madden, Wasik, & Petza, 1989) completing its language curriculum. The reading instruction is provided in small groups for all students. They receive instruction for 90 min every day in one block of time, and the reading groups are based on reading levels. The instruction utilizes cooperative learning, provides for reading assessments every 8 weeks, provides reading tutors when needed, and requires a *program facilitator* on the school campus. The facilitator is viewed by the SFA developers as central to the success of the program and the position requires significant training. The facilitator provides ongoing professional development for teachers, coordinates the school's family support team, and organizes the ongoing 8-week assessments for each student.

Slavin and Madden (1999) provide ample data supporting the success of this program relative to similar control schools including that children tend to do better in middle school relative to their non-SFA counterparts. However, not all children did well. The findings indicate that 15% of SFA third graders were approximately a year behind grade level and about 4% were 2 years behind (Madden, Slavin, Karweit, Dolan, & Wasik, 1993). Although children who were struggling readers were provided one-to-one tutoring, this was for only 20 min a day, and the tutoring was more reading practice focused rather than utilizing a more skill-building approach. In addition, there was no shift in programs or interventions. Obviously, with these sorts of numbers it seems likely that many, if not most, of the children who did not respond to SFA have some type of language disorder and dyslexia.

DISTAR (Engelmann & Bruner, 1983) is included here due to the number of programs it makes available and the change in teaching approaches it recommends. Although not as thoroughly school-wide as SFA, DISTAR like SFA was also designed for beginning readers (grades 1–3) who came from disadvantaged backgrounds. It was part of Project Follow-Through, a federally funded project undertaken in 1968. DISTAR was one of nine approaches to be investigated to see how effective they were in serving these youth. DISTAR is currently published by McGraw Hill and is marketed under the title of *Scientific Research Associates (SRA): Direct Instruction Programs.*

The goal of DISTAR's originators was to create a program, which with relatively minimal additional training could be provided by teachers to their students to get better and more consistent results from their teaching. This is in part due to the teachers having to learn and to teach from a script meant to enhance consistency of practice, similar to utilizing a training manual. Since 1968, there have been a number of research studies supporting the effectiveness of the direct instruction curricula (e.g., Gersten, Darch, & Gleason, 1988; Gersten, Woodward, & Darch, 1986; Meyer, Gersten, & Gutkin, 1983) including a meta-analysis published in 1996 that reviewed the prior 25 years of DISTAR research (Adams & Engelmann, 1996). In terms of the training, teachers are required to take a 1 week preservice workshop with additional training/supervision of 1–2 h a week to implement the programs. There is no coordinator job, per se, as with SFA, but ongoing training and supervision are essential aspects to the mastering of DISTAR. In one study (Meyer et al.), their *project manager* spent up to 40 days a year at the model school sites.

The amount of time taken for instruction is in large part dependent upon the number of programs and the intensity of instruction to be provided. If just the reading program is provided, the minimum amount of instruction and practice is typically about 1 h. However, if the reading, math, and language programs are all used, the amount of time taken could be up to 60% of the school day (Meyer et al., 1983).

Relative to SFA, concerns have been expressed about the relative lack of instruction in written expression (Uhry & Clark, 2004), the modified orthography used in the early stages of the reading program (Bartlett, 1979), and the negative impact on teacher creativity due to the heavily scripted nature of the intervention (American Federation of Teachers, 1999). Finally, Torgesen (2004), in commenting on both DISTAR and SFA, remarked that both were useful for at-risk students, but were not as useful for the more disabled readers.

Curriculum

As illustrated in Table 7.1, there are a variety of reading programs that have a research base. For this book, three different types of curricula are discussed. The first type will be those curricula that have an organized/structured, well-sequenced series of experiences that have some research support and can be adopted by schools to provide prevention and some beginning intervention to their regular education students. This will fit in with the new *IDEIA* tier model, but are not as MSLE oriented. This first group is sometimes referred to as comprehensive, core reading programs. These programs by design cover the fundamentals outlined in the scientifically based reading research (SBRR; Snow, Burns, & Griffin, 1998): phonemic awareness, phonics, fluency, vocabulary, and comprehension. Examples of this type of program are the *Open Court Reading* (2002) and the *A Legacy of Literacy* (2003) programs, both adopted by the state of California as basal curricula for beginning readers.

Table 7.1 Intensive intervention multicomponent reading programs with a research base

Intervention	Target students	Instructional grouping	Research base
Corrective reading	Grade levels 4–5	4–5 students to the whole class	Beck, Perfetti, and McKeown (1982), Borman, Hewes, Overman, and Brown (2002), Foorman et al. (1998), Fuchs, Fuchs, and Maxwell (1988), Gregory, Hackney, and Gregory (1982), Hasbrouck and Tindal (1992), Vitale, Medland, Romance, and Weaver (1993)
Language!	Reading levels primary to ninth grade	Small groups of 3–5 students	Greene (1996)
Project read	A primary 3 sets of materials and a 4–12 sets of reading materials	Small group or whole class	Bruce and Salzman (2002), Bruce, Snodgrass, and Salzman (1999), Enfield (1976), Stoner (1991)
Success for all	Grades K-3	Small group or whole class	Ross, Smith, and Casey (1997), Slavin and Madden (2000), Slavin, Madden, Karweit, Livermon, and Dolan (1990)
Wilson Reading System	Grades 2–12	Small group, 3–5	Banks, Guyer, and Guyer (1993), Bursuck and Dickson (1999), O'Connor and Wilson (1995), Wood (2002)

Adapted from the Florida Center for Reading Research. Please note this is not an approved list of programs. We make a distinction here between research based and evidence based. Since the National Reading Panel's report on the issues that need to be addressed in a curriculum, a number of new programs have been developed according to those guidelines but do not have independent research report but refer to themselves as evidence based

The second type are those that focus on working with students who are struggling readers, usually one or more years behind and experiencing a great range of reading skills. Although there is often a dyslexic subpopulation among these students, they are not designed specifically for students who require special education. One of these programs has a more MSLE orientation, the *Wilson Program* (Wilson, 1988a, 1988b), while the other, the *Language!* (Greene, 1996) program, although often dealing with similar populations does not have the MSLE focus.

Finally, the third group, often referred to as supplemental intervention programs, is designed for students whose needs are more specific. Examples of these programs are the *Lindamood Phoneme Sequencing* program for training in phonemic awareness and decoding (LiPS: also formerly entitled Auditory Discrimination in Depth); *Great Leaps for Reading*, which targets primarily reading fluency; and *Visualizing/ Verbalizing*, which targets reading comprehension.

The review of all curricula available to practitioners is beyond the scope of this book. For more information about other programs, both core and remedially oriented, the Florida Center for Reading Research (http://www.fcrr.org) has reviewed over 120 programs. For those readers more specifically interested in MSLE-oriented programs, Uhry and Clark (2004) have reviewed a number of other popular multisensory programs and is a useful resource. The three programs examined in this chapter provide school-based personnel with examples of the types of programs available and the kinds of approaches, trainings, and/or commitments the school would need to make to adopt these programs.

NICHD helped establish the usefulness of the *Open Court* program as it served as one of the interventions at one of the sites utilized by Reid Lyon and his colleagues. This particular site was in Texas and the researchers found that when *Open Court* was used, which they (Foorman, Francis, Fletcher, Schatschneider, & Mehta, 1998) referred to as their *direct code* method, comparing it to the *embedded* and *implicit code* approaches, students fared significantly better in word reading when taught the direct code approach.

This finding has not gone without controversy. Others have argued that the Texas study had methodological and other flaws (Coles, 2000; Moustafa & Land, 2002). However, the Foorman et al. (1998) study is not the only data available supporting *Open Court's* usefulness. Although a potential conflict of interest, McGraw-Hill did commission what they referred to as an independent consultant to review data from three cohorts of schools in California comparing *Open Court* using schools with matched schools not using *Open Court* (McRae, 2002). This study also supported the basic finding of the Foorman et al. study "that students attending schools using *Open Court* materials acquired basic reading skills at a faster rate than students attending demographically similar schools not using *Open Court* materials" (p. 21).

Although the *A Legacy of Literacy* curriculum does not have similar data available to it and is not so specifically surrounded by controversy, it generally meets the same standards and was chosen by California as an alternative to *Open Court*. Some of the advantages of these comprehensive, core reading programs are that they are in a structure familiar to most teachers, provide significant support in terms of materials, demand little extra specialized learning/knowledge, and are designed in ways that fit nicely into a tiered model approach to instruction. Although there is research suggesting that every curriculum needs a good teacher to make it work (e.g., Taylor, Pearson, Clark, & Walpole, 2000; Tivnan & Hemphill, 2004), it is also true that over 75% of teachers surveyed about how they teach reading reported that they all relied on a comprehensive, core reading program as at least a building block to their instruction in reading (as cited in Al Otaiba, Kosanovich-Grek, Torgesen,

Housler, & Wahl, 2005). Overall, this makes these programs relatively cost effective in terms of the amount of financial resources needed for teachers to learn how to use the product. It also reduces time and/or financial resources in instruction and support for teachers, and aids in effective instructional strategies. This in turn reduces the number of children who would have required further instructional and/ or special educational support at a later point in their educational career.

The Wilson Method and *Language!* are examples of two of the more remedially oriented curricula, which were selected for review in this book in part because of the support that they have both received over the last few years from IDA, and in part due to the number of public and private special education schools that have been adopting them.

The *Wilson Reading System* (Wilson, 2002) was developed for struggling readers initially targeting dyslexic students and was designed within the MSLE framework, although its use is being expanded to below grade level and English language learning students. It is a well-structured, well-sequenced curriculum that meets MSLE and SBBR standards and is currently serving students in 2nd through 12th grades. Although originally developed as an intensive remedial intervention program for individuals or small instructional groups, it is also now being used for instruction, still primarily in small groups, but within the larger classroom format. When used remedially, it typically requires 1–1.5 h per day for instruction and is completed by a Wilson-certified instructor. When used more instructionally, the program is more often taught by a remedial reading teacher or a regular classroom teacher. The program integrates reading and writing and, especially for remedial purposes, suggests that the multisensory training that goes along with the program is essential for success.

Teacher training is more rigorous than the aforementioned approaches. After an initial 3-day overview, teachers are required to take a 6-CEU online course from the training center with occasional/as needed follow-up supervisory site visits over the first year of implementation. When completed, the teacher is considered a Level 1 Wilson trained instructor. A Level II trained instructor is required to have a Level I certification plus an additional year's course. Barbara Wilson and her colleagues suggest that if the Wilson System is adopted the school district or private school should develop a within system Wilson trainer. There is a significant increase in time and finances invested by schools/districts who want to train teachers in this system.

Initial evidence exists that is supportive of the Wilson program as an effective intervention program for students with reading difficulties (Banks, Guyer, & Guyer, 1993; Bursuck & Dickson, 1999; Wilson & O'Connor, 1995). The *Wilson Reading System* was also one of four programs selected, including *Corrective Reading* (Engelmann, Meyer, Johnson & Carnine, 1999; Engelmann, Carnine, & Johnson, 1999; Engelmann, Meyer, et al., 1999), *Failure Free Reading* (Lockavitch, 1996), and *Spell Read Phonological Auditory Training* (P.A.T.; MacPhee, 1990), to be part of a longitudinal study on reading intervention funded by the Haan Foundation and referred to as Power4Kids (http://www.haan4kids.org/power4kids). Its first year's findings (Torgesen, 2006) have recently been made available. Effect sizes across all programs are small to medium; from the available data the Wilson and *Spell Read P.A.T.* seem to be producing more consistent results with results on basic reading skills being somewhat more powerful than on comprehension (at least given the ways that these skills are being measured in the study). Much more data are being collected and these should be considered as preliminary findings.

The *Language!* program is also a comprehensive curriculum focusing on the same skill set as the *Wilson Reading Program.* It has been adopted by an increasing number of school districts for delayed readers, often regardless of whether the students are identified as eligible for special education. It was originally developed for delayed readers in middle and high school, and can be used as either a comprehensive or a supplemental program. It is referred to as a comprehensive literacy program that integrates reading, writing, and other language arts skills with material developed for grades 3–12. It is designed to be administered in small, flexible instructional groups, which are paced over two daily sessions totaling 90 min per day. It comprised what Greene refers to as 16 *language strands* from phonemic awareness to reading comprehension and from spelling to sentence and paragraph structure. Each set of lessons moves from the simpler to the more complex (i.e., from phonemic awareness and/or decoding, to fluency, and to comprehending connected text). As previously noted, this follows the neural networking model described by Berninger (Berninger & Richards, 2002).

Recommended teacher training consists of a 3-day training for Level 1 (grades 1–3) followed by ongoing support and a 2-day training for Level 2. The publishers stress that ongoing support is essential for successful implementation. Teachers are supported through a resource guide that offers many materials designed to enhance instruction with detailed lesson plans. Although it is becoming rapidly adopted across the country, the only research evidence is Greene's study (1996). Program evaluations have been conducted in Baldwin County, Alabama; Sacramento, California; and Idaho Falls, Idaho; and all tended to be positive. Nevertheless, further empirical support is needed.

The *Language!* program's thoroughness is clearly one of the major attractions for school districts as most school districts choose to utilize it for both struggling regular education students and students who require special education. One district, known to the authors, uses this program as a Tier 2 intervention in a small class of 12 and as a Tier 3 intervention in groups of four or fewer. In an email from the publishers, they had no official comment about whether they thought this was a good practice model and said that they thought that these kinds of decisions were best left to local districts. Here, as with *Wilson,* the publishers note that teacher training and support is essential to insure appropriate implementation. Although *Language!* is not a multisensory intervention, it is a rather complicated program. We have observed that these programs can work both preventively and remedially, but that the teacher training, the number of students in the group, and the intensity are extremely important to the student's success. As with most successful programs, they can only reach maximum benefit with concomitant treatment integrity.

Supplemental Intervention Reading Programs

As illustrated in Table 7.2 there are a variety of more narrowly focused programs that have a research base. There are a number of programs designed as more specific skill-based interventions, and again the Florida Center for Reading Research is a good place to get a more complete overview of the full range of these programs. In this chapter, we selected for review programs that illustrate each of the areas that the National Reading Panel suggested were important. Specifically, in the areas of phonemic awareness and decoding, *Phoneme Sequencing Program for Reading, Spelling, and Speech* (3rd ed.; LiPS: Lindamood & Lindamood, 1998), in the area of reading fluency, *Great Leaps* (Mercer, Campbell, Miller, Mercer, & Lane, 2000), and in the area of reading comprehension, *Visualization and Verbalization* (Bell, 1986). A sample of other more narrowly focused programs that address phonemic awareness and phonics are summarized in Table 7.2.

LiPS is a multisensory program originally created by Charles and Patricia Lindamood in the early 1970s and was then called Auditory Discrimination in Depth,

Table 7.2 More narrowly focused intensive intervention programs: Phonemic awareness and phonics

Intervention	Target students	Instructional grouping	Research base
Lexia	Phonic-based reading: Grades K to 3 Strategies for older Students (SOS): Ages 9-years to adult		McCabe (2002), Stevens (2000)
Phono-Graphix	Students grades 1–5	One-to-one or small group instruction Has been used to teach large groups.	Curran, Guin, and Marshall (2002), Denton, Fletcher, Anthony, and Francis (2006), Fill, Gips, and Hosty (1998), McGuinness and McGuinness (1999), McGuinness, McGuinness, and McGuinness (1996)
Read, write, and type	Ages 6–9 years		Read, write & type! (n.d.), Spanish-speaking Primary Students (n.d.), Torgesen, Wagner, Rashotte, and Herron (n.d.)

Adapted from the Florida Center for Reading Research. Please note this is not an approved list of programs or ADD. LiPS is the third edition of this program and was revised by Patricia Lindamood (a speech pathologist) and her daughter Phyllis Lindamood. Patricia's original training emerges in the treatment intervention in that a significant portion of the multisensory orientation is oromotor, or getting the students to attend to their articulation and mouth formations in the development of their phonemic awareness. Part of the premise is that the encoding of the phonemes is facilitated by proper production.

The current program, although it can be administered to small classrooms or groups, is most often offered remedially in a one-to-one treatment situation. The Lindamoods have always espoused that remedial treatment should be intensive, which is generally described as a minimum of 2 h, preferably 4–6 h over a 6–8 week program. It takes the student through phonemic awareness, to alphabetics, and to syllabication/structural analysis with some sight word development.

LiPS is one of, if not the most, researched and well documented of the multisensory approaches (e.g., Alexandra, Anderson, Heilman, Voeller, & Torgesen, 1991; Kennedy & Backman, 1993; Sadoski & Willson, 2006; Torgesen, Wagner et al., 1999, Torgesen, Alexander et al., 2001). LiPS' impact on neurological functioning as established by pre- and post-treatment fMRI research is well documented (e.g., Adair et al., 2000; Eden et al., 2004; Simos et al., 2002). In general, what is known is that LiPS has been found to exceed or do as well as embedded phonics programs, tending to do better on word analysis skills and found to be slightly, but not statistically significantly, better in reading comprehension depending upon the reading measures used. In addition, LiPS has performed significantly better than the more standard core reading programs used for the typical control groups. Improvements in fMRI functions post-treatment also substantiate the effects of LiPS and offer further assurance that significant change has occurred.

In terms of the teacher training required for administering this program, a 3-day workshop is required along with the purchase of the materials. The more substantive "expense" of LiPS is related to the fact that the best results were associated with one-on-one or very small group instruction, with intensive implementation that is not yet standard practice in most public school systems. However, it is important to acknowledge that as a child gets to Tier 3 with little gain, the data suggest that remediation really needs to be intensive to "close the gap."

Reading fluency has a history of being harder to remediate than word accuracy (Shaywitz, 2003). There are a number of programs available, most of which are of the re-reading variety, like *Read Naturally*, and these repeated reading approaches have had some documented impact (Meyer & Felton, 1999). A recent meta-analysis found that goal setting and feedback should be part of any fluency intervention (Morgan & Sideridis, 2006). A program that Shaywitz described as "responsible for bringing about these impressive gains" (Shaywitz, p. 272) in reading fluency was *Great Leaps*. Developed by Kenneth Campbell (1996), a special education teacher, this program was initially researched by Cecil Mercer, a long-time Florida reading researcher (Mercer et al., 2000). Mercer and colleagues found that the program had a significant impact on reading fluency for middle school students with specific learning disabilities. Again, although not dyslexic students per se, most are likely to have been dyslexic. Besides just increasing the speed of one's reading, others (e.g., Fuchs, Fuchs, Hosp, & Jenkins, 2001) have also pointed out the significant correlation between fluency and reading comprehension.

As Shaywitz further pointed out, fluency training is usually done in a brief period, everyday, for months. *Great Leaps* was designed as a supplementary program and is typically provided to students in one less than 10-min practice session per day. It does not meet SBBR criteria, as it is for fluency only. Teachers, paraprofessionals, and parents can administer the lessons. Training is by videos and/or a trainer and the trainers are very responsive to email questions. The authors have used it with parents providing the tutorial support to keep a child involved in the reading process.

Using this program, three types of information are quickly read by students: phonics, phrases/sentences, and stories. The student's progress is graphed, visually representing the progress of the student and the graph then becomes a goal-setting tool as well. On his website (http://www.greatleaps.com), Campbell (n.d.) does offer an FAQ caveat question about how much progress students can make. His response is that "Great Leaps brings children to an independent level of reading – this may, or may not be at grade level" (p. 9). Yet, the program fulfills Berninger's criteria (Berninger & Richards, 2002) of getting subroutines "firing" in connected time to promote neural links, and it meets the Morgan and Sideridis' (2006) criteria of providing goals and feedback all of which are positives. In conclusion, it is important to acknowledge that while *Great Leaps* is still in the position of needing much more empirical research to support, it appears to be a theoretically sound intervention.

For the final area, reading comprehension, *Visualization/Verbalization* (V/V) was selected as we believe it to be a solid supplemental intervention program. As reviewed earlier in the NRP's Report, there are a number of strategies that have been found helpful to promote reading comprehension. There is also a history in the literature of visualization strategies being helpful for language and reading comprehension (e.g., Chan, Cole, & Morris, 1990; Zimmerman, 2004). Nancy Bell (1986) developed V/V as *Visualizing and verbalizing for language comprehension and thinking*, and it became a part of the Lindamood-Bell Learning Processes (LBLP) programs.

Bell (1991) describes the theory behind the intervention in an article discussing gestalt imagery as a critical factor in language comprehension. Studies have also supported that V/V as its own program, and part of the broader set of LBLP programs has been found to produce significant gains in reading comprehension relative to more traditional programs (Johnson-Glenberg, 2000; Sadoski & Willson, 2006). The program is designed for multiple settings although small groups and individuals are the most common formats. The program requires a 2-day training for teachers to implement the program. The instructor uses direct questions to help a student form images utilizing structure words (e.g., shape, color) that provide a framework that helps the student talk about a story and to begin to form mental images of the story that the student then begins to see. Theoretically, it can be incorporated into other programs or can provide stand-alone instruction.

Controversial Intervention Strategies

Controversial intervention strategies have been with us throughout history and they have covered a plethora of disorders. These treatments are generally considered to be *nonstandard* alternatives to the therapies or interventions most accepted in the given field. Sometimes, they can be found to be effective at a later time, but at the given moment we do not have the research to document such efficacy. Sometimes, they can be relatively harmless, except for taking away time from what a more research-based program might be able to do, and sometimes they can be harmful. This chapter will focus on those interventions that are typically not viewed as *primary* interventions for dyslexia even though some may have somewhat of a research base, to those that have some anecdotal evidence, but no empirical research base. Common to each of the controversial interventions discussed is that all have some national recognition and at least some "fan" support.

There are a number of programs that exist that will not be reviewed here, and again the Florida Center for Reading Research is a good Web site to visit to see what is known and the website www.quackwatch.com can be useful to try to find out the degree to which the claims of a particular program are substantiated. This chapter reviews three programs that purport to address issues of auditory processing: *Fast ForWord- Language* (Miller & Tallal, 1996), *Earobics* (Cognitive Concepts, 2000), and Tomatis (1978). This chapter also reviews two programs that focus on vision: *Irlen lenses* (Irlen, 1983) and optometric visual training (Rayner, 1998; Taylor, 1965). Finally, we look at two relatively well-advertised programs, the *Davis Method* (Davis & Braun, 1997, 2003) and the *Dore Program* (Dore & Rutherford, 2001).

Auditory Processing

Fast ForWord (Scientific Learning Corporation, 1999) is a computer-based program that utilizes acoustically modified speech in an attempt to enhance auditory processing. The theory underlying the approach has been explicated by Tallal and her colleagues (Merzenich et al., 1996; Tallal et al., 1996). There have been a number of fMRI intervention studies on *Fast ForWord* (e.g., Agnew, Dorn, & Eden, 2003; Lajiness-O'Neill, Akamine, & Bowyer, in press; Simos et al., 2002) documenting that significant neurological changes occur when students with dyslexia complete the program and that the changes are such that the child's neural processing better approximates the comparison student's processing. Where the conflict arises is whether changes in reading skills take place.

One recent study (Gaab, Gabrielli, Deutsch, Tallal, & Temple, 2007) has documented improved reading scores, while earlier studies either do or do not find any differences with other intervention methods (e.g., Agnew, Dorn, & Eden, 2004; Hook, Macaruso, & Jones, 2001). It would seem that we can clearly state that aspects of auditory/neurological processing are altered by *Fast ForWord*, but it is less clear how significantly reading skills are impacted. This concern is also being addressed by the Scientific Learning Company as they have expanded their product base and the "old" *Fast ForWord* is now called *Fast ForWord-Language* and their newer program, for which we have been unable to find any empirical research, is *Fast ForWord-Reading*.

Earobics (n.d.) is another auditory training program that describes itself as a multisensory intervention program. It consists of an interactive software program and teacher guides. On its website, it is described as a "proven, research based intervention solution" (Earobics Solutions, n.d., p. 1) However, they have no list of empirical data available on their website, and only one study was located regarding its efficacy. The Pokorni study (Porkorni, Worthington, & Jamison, 2004) did find that *Earobics* produced significant gains in phoneme segmentation, but not on other language measures or on reading-related measures. They suggest that further study is needed to support the notion that it is useful for dyslexia.

Alfred Tomatis (1978), a French otolaryngologist, presented his program in his book *Education and Dyslexia.* He claimed that listening exercises focused on classical music, and Gregorian chants can remediate the linguistic processing issues that students with learning disorders face. Although more popular in Canada, there are Tomatis Centers throughout the United States. We found a meta-analytic review of five earlier "applied" studies (Gilmor, 1999) and a later study that was a follow-up/longitudinal study to one of the studies in the meta-analysis (Kershner, Cummings, Clarke, Hadfield, & Kershner, 1986, 1990). In the meta-analysis that looked at five different areas: linguistic, psycho-motor, personal and social adjustment, cognitive, and auditory, small to medium effect sizes, 0.30–0.41, were found on the first four areas. But interestingly, the effect size for the auditory area was only 0.04. In addition, there were no measures of reading. On the other study noted, there was no statistically significant difference above and beyond the standard treatment and in this study reading was included. Consequently, it would be appropriate to consider it still unproven at this time.

Visual Processing

Irlen Lenses, sometimes referred to as tinted lenses, is a procedure developed by Helen Irlen (1983) and presented at the 91st annual convention of the American Psychological Association. She proposed that "scotopic sensitivity" is a visual defect that is created by difficulties with things like light source, glare, luminance, wave length, and black/white contrast. She suggested that these issues with vision can create reading problems and that scotopic sensitivity often coexisted with dyslexia. She claims that via a specialized screening whereby the student is vision tested utilizing seven different tints, colored lenses, or overlays, the precise tint to ameliorate the scotopic sensitivity can be chosen. Glasses or overlays of that particular tint are then used to enable the student to read better (Irlen, 2005).

The *Journal of Learning Disabilities* did a special issue on Irlen Lenses and of the articles, three (Blaskey et al., 1990; O'Connor, Sofo, Kendall, & Olsen 1990; Robinson & Conway, 1990) had an evaluation component, but none was empirical. The Blaskey and colleagues' study found no reading improvement; O'Connor and colleagues found some improvement, however, nonparametrics were used and the comparisons were only gain vs. no gain without any clear way to gauge degree of impact; and the Robinson and Conway study used no randomization or control groups. The summary presentation in that issue (Parker, 1990), as well as a later summarization of the research on the lenses (Chaban, n.d.), suggests that studies "supporting" the lenses are rife with methodological concerns and generate inconclusive results.

Probably the most reasoned argument available is by Evans (1999) who states that even if lenses can be helpful for "visual" processing, they clearly will not ameliorate the phonological problems that underlie most cases of dyslexia. The American Academy of Pediatrics (1998) has also issued a statement that learning disabilities cannot be improved by the use of colored lenses. Clinically speaking, however, in a personal communication with Dr. Frank Grisham, former clinical director of the University of California Optometric Center, he stated that his observations are that what an overlay can sometimes do is reduce glare to overly sensitive children preventing eye strain and headaches, but cannot improve reading skills.

Other visual processing interventions have also been proposed. Concerns about refractive errors, eye muscle tracking, convergence, and strabismus are real. Ophthalmologists usually will diagnose and correct these when possible, but then tend to refer to special education for reading intervention (Keys, 2001). However, there is another field, often referred to as developmental optometrics, which is also an established field. Developmental optometrics proposes a number of intervention programs to "treat" these kinds of difficulties (which some believe are a "cause" of reading problems) via a variety of optometric exercises.

As noted in Chap. 2, the American Academy of Ophthalmology (2001) has issued a statement concluding that "there appears to be no consistent evidence that supports behavioral vision therapy, orthoptic vision therapy, or colored overlays and lenses as effective treatments for learning disabilities" (p. 1). The American Academy of Pediatrics (1998) has also issued a similar statement. However, the controversy remains. For example, Marrs and Patrick (2002) make a strong case for the *Reading Plus Program* developed by Taylor Associates (who also developed the *Visagraph II* eye-movement recording systems). We believe that a large part of the more recent confusion can be attributed to what some of these new "vision" programs are actually doing, or having students do. If we look at some of the interventions, such as this guided reading program, we see that the training is a form of reading fluency training, usually a re-reading methodology, which can be helpful. However, it is not the machinery or the optical instrument that we believe is helpful, but rather the training's accompanying actual fluency training.

Other Programs

The *Davis Method* (Davis & Braun, 1997, 2003) is a California-based program that is gaining more recognition nationally. It is based on Ronald Davis' self-discovery of his own "dyslexia" and its cure as an adult. However, he has also related that he was thought of as a retarded child and could have been viewed today as a child with autistic symptoms; so, the "symptom" picture is a bit confusing. We could not find any empirical data on this system. Without going into the details of the intervention, it is clear that visualization and tactile work with clay are central parts of the treatment. One of the most significant problems of this intervention is that "actual teaching to read or even teaching to learn seems absent from the Davis methods" (Cicci, 2001, p. 11). This program has not been reviewed by the Florida Center for Reading Research.

Finally, the Dore Program, or as it is also called in Britain and Australia, the *Dyslexia Dyspraxia Attention Treatment Progamme* (DDAT), has been receiving attention in the press and in advertising about its role in "curing" a variety of disorders, but primarily dyslexia. The claim is that this program is based on the "cerebellar deficit hypothesis" (Nicolson, Fawcett, & Dean, 2001). It is argued that dyslexic students have a significant difficulty in making skills automatic, thereby not being able to develop fluent skills to the point where there is no need for conscious effort. The goal then is to retrain the cerebellum utilizing a variety of repetitive physical activities, balancing exercises, etc. to enhance reading skills. We found one study and a 2-year follow up to that initial study (Reynolds & Nicolson, 2006; Reynolds, Nicolson, & Hambly, 2003) that tried to evaluate whether this exercise-based approach was a useful treatment. The studies concluded that there were gains from DDAT, primarily in vestibular and visual functioning, but also in phonemic awareness, but not in reading per se. Others (International Dyslexia Association, 2004; Rack, Snowling, Hulme, & Gibbs, 2007) have challenged the research on a variety of methodological, neurological, and educational grounds. It seems safe to conclude that at this time more research is needed before the Dore Achievers Centers (http://www.doreusa.com) should be considered a front-line intervention for dyslexia.

Concluding Comments

School professionals in general, and school psychologists in particular, can play an important role in discussing alternative interventions when parents ask for information or advice in making decisions. Promoting communication and collaboration between parents, medical providers, and school personnel is important in helping parents make well-informed decisions about choosing treatments for their children. Providing support to parents by reading and discussing information about evidence-based and alternative treatments can be very helpful. The focus in this book, however, is to try to promote evidence-based programs both to parents and other school personnel. We can also encourage parents and other school personnel to take advantage of participating in well-designed studies of new interventions as they develop alternative therapies if parents are interested. But we also believe that it is important to remember that moving to an alternative therapy before trying any of the more evidence-based programs available, even if it does not seem like the alternative intervention is not likely to do harm, does in its own way create the potential for harm. It takes time away from treatments that may have a greater likelihood for success and for being able to "close the gap" sooner, which we already know is important. Further, in most instances, any time we put a student in a program that does not work for that student, it impacts motivation and may even impact the student's feelings of being unable to be helped.

Appendix

Resources on Dyslexia

Valuable Information on the Internet

The Internet can be an important tool for families, teachers, and practitioners seeking information on Dyslexia and related topics. The vast amount of information that can be retrieved in any given search, however, can also make it a time-consuming and unwieldy resource. Some useful Web sites are listed as follows. The list is by no means exhaustive, but it contains links to some of the most valuable Web-based materials that are currently available.

Assessment and Intervention

Florida Center for Reading Research

http://www.fcrr.org
   The Florida Center for Reading Research (FCRR) is affiliated with Florida State University. The center Web site has resources for teachers, parents, administrators, and researchers. The site provides detailed reports on many different assessment programs. Reports include information on implementing the intervention.

National Research Center on Learning Disabilities

http://www.nrcld.org
   The National Research Center on Learning Disabilities (NRCLD) Web site provides evidence on research-based practices in both identification and intervention for students with learning disabilities. Their site is useful to educators, policy makers, and parents. This site also provides excellent resources on response-to-intervention (RTI) models.

Vaughn Gross Center for Reading and Language Arts

http://www.texasreading.org/utcrla/
 The Vaughn Gross Center is active in both ongoing research projects and translating research findings into practice. The center focuses on reading and mathematics instruction and provides online professional development as well as guidelines for instruction and intervention based on current research findings.

What Works Clearinghouse: Institute for Education Sciences

http://ies.ed.gov/ncee/wwc/
 The What Works Clearinghouse (WWC) is a part of the Institute for Education Sciences, a federal government entity. The WWC provides reviews of instruction and intervention that apply rigorous standards of scientific research outlined by the federal government. Information on curricula and programs in a variety of areas (reading, mathematics, early childhood education, dropout prevention) is provided. This is a good source for locating results of rigorous scientific evaluations of various programs.

Institute for the Development of Educational Achievement

http://idea.uoregon.edu/
 The Institute for the Development of Educational Achievement engages in both research and dissemination of findings on a variety of topics related to the academic and social well being of children and youth. Specific to dyslexia, the site provides reviews of assessments and curricula for reading.

National Reading Panel

http://www.nationalreadingpanel.org/
 This Web site provides the findings of the National Reading Panel in regard to reading instruction and intervention. In addition, the site provides numerous materials for teachers, parents, and other educators regarding reading instruction.

National Center on Student Progress Monitoring

http://www.studentprogress.org/
 This site provides extensive information on methods for monitoring student progress in attainment of academic skills, particularly in reading and mathematics. The site reviews many commonly available tools for reading assessment.

Broader Research-Based Practice

National Association of State Directors of Special Education

http://nasdse.org/

The National Association of State Directors of Special Education (NASDSE) Web site is a general source for information regarding special education. Particularly relevant to reading instruction and identification of students with reading disabilities is the series of blueprints for implementation of RTI.

Special Education Resources on the Internet

http://www.seriweb.com

The Special Education Resources on the Internet (SERI) Web site provides links to resources on the Internet that provide information related to special education topics. The site is organized according to general topics and is easy to navigate. However, SERI provides no information on the quality of the resources listed.

US Department of Education

http://www.ed.gov/

This is the main entry site to the US Department of Education's Internet resources. From here, one can navigate to all other sites within the department such as the Office of Special Education and Rehabilitation or links related to IDEIA (2004).

IDEIA Partnership

http://www.ideapartnership.org

The IDEA Partnership is a collaboration of organizations involved in work with children and youth with disabilities. The purpose of the organization is to provide opportunities for collaborative work among these agencies and other service personnel.

Parent-Friendly Resources

International Dyslexia Association

http://www.interdys.org

The Web site of the International Dyslexia Association provides extensive resources for parents, community members, educators, and researchers. The site provides concise information sheets as well as links to more extensive material. The site also provides information about conferences, training opportunities, and local branches.

Learning Disabilities Association of America

http://www.ldanatl.org/
   The Learning Disabilities Association of America (LDA) Web site provides information on all learning disabilities. The site is useful for both educators and parents. Fact sheets, FAQs, and lengthier publications are available at this website: many of them at no cost.

LD OnLine

http://www.ldonline.org/
   LD OnLine has many resources for parents, educators, researchers, and students with learning disabilities. The site provides very accessible articles on topics such as dyslexia and high school students, IDEA, writing goals, and strategies for helping students stay organized.

National Center for Learning Disabilities

http://www.ncld.org/
   The National Center for Learning Disabilities (NCLD) Web site provides information about learning disabilities for parents and educators. The site addresses issues of learning disabilities across the life span and also provides information on legislation and other advocacy issues.

National Dissemination Center for Children with Disabilities

http://www.nichcy.org
   The National Dissemination Center for Children with Disabilities' purpose is to serve as a central source of information on disabilities, IDEA, No Child Left Behind (as it relates to children with disabilities) and research-based information on effective educational practices. There are resources in Spanish as well as English, and the site provides direct access to support personnel.

Reading Rockets

http://www.readingrockets.org/
   Reading Rockets is focused on "launching young readers." As a consequence, there are many useful resources for both parents and teachers who work with young

children. The focus is on the development of pre-reading and reading skills in young children from birth through the early primary years. Resources include presentations on early reading for parents and educators. Most of the parent materials are also available in Spanish.

Schwab Learning

http://www.schwablearning.org

Schwab Learning is primarily geared toward parents who have children with disabilities. There are resources on identifying possible disabilities, helping children to manage school, resources, and other important topics.

References

A *Legacy of Literacy* (2003). Boston, MA: Houghton Mifflin Co.

Ackerman, P. T., & Dykman, R. A. (1993). Phonological processes, immediate memory, and confrontational naming in dyslexia. *Journal of Learning Disabilities*, 26, 597–609.

Ackerman, P., Dykman, R., & Gardner, M. (1990). Counting rate, naming rate, phonological sensitivity and memory span: Major factors in dyslexia. *Journal of Learning Disabilities*, 23, 325–327.

Ackerman, P. T., Holloway, C. A., Youngdahl, P. L., & Dykman, R. A. (2001). The double-deficit theory of reading disability does not fit all. *Learning Disabilities Research and Practice*, 16, 152–160.

Adair, J., Nadeau, S., Conway, T., Gonzalez-Rothe, L., Heilman, P., Gruen, I., & Heilman, K. (2000). Alteration of functional anatomy of reading induced by rehabilitation of an alexic patient. *Neuropsychiatry, Neuropsychology, and Behavioral Neurology*, 13, 303–311.

Adams, G. L., & Engelmann, S. (1996). *Research on direct instruction: 25 years beyond DISTAR*. Seattle, WA: Educational Achievement Systems.

Adams, M. J. (1990). *Beginning to read: Thinking and learning about print*. Cambridge, MA: MIT Press.

Agnew, J. A., Dorn, C., & Eden, G. F. (2004). Effect of intensive training on auditory processing and reading skills. *Brain and Language*, 88, 21–25.

Alexandra, A., Anderson, H., Heilman, P., Voeller, K., & Torgesen, J. (1991). Phonological awareness training in the reeducation of analytic decoding deficits in a group of severe dyslexics. *Annals of Dyslexia*, 41, 193–206.

Alho, O. P. (1990). The validity of questionnaire reports of a history of acute otitis media. *American Journal of Epidemiology*, 132, 1–7.

Al Otaiba, S., & Fuchs, D. (2002). Characteristics of children who are unresponsive to early literacy intervention. *Remedial & Special Education*, 23, 300–317.

Al Otaiba, S., & Fuchs, D. (2006). Who are the young children for whom best practices in reading are ineffective? An experimental and longitudinal study. *Journal of Learning Disabilities*, 39, 414–431.

Al Otaiba, S., Kosanovich-Grek, M. L., Torgesen, J. K., Housler, L., & Wahl, M. (2005). Reviewing core kindergarten programs and first-grade reading programs in light of No Child Left Behind: An exploratory study. *Reading and Writing Quarterly*, 21, 377–400.

Allor, J. H. (2002). The relationships of phonemic awareness and rapid naming to reading development. *Learning Disability Quarterly*, 25, 47.

American Academy of Ophthalmology (2001, September). *Complementary therapy assessment: Vision therapy for learning disabilities*. Retrieved August 2007, http://www.regence.com/trgmedpol/alliedHealth/ah19.html

American Academy of Pediatrics, American Academy of Ophthalmology, & American Association for Pediatric Ophthalmology and Strabismus. (1998). Learning disabilities, dyslexia, and vision: A subject review. *Pediatrics*, 102, 1217–1219.

American Federation of Teachers. (July). *Building on the best, learning from what works: Five promising remedial programs*. Washington, DC: American Federation of Teachers.

American Psychiatric Association. (2000). *Diagnostic and statistical manual of mental disorders* (4th ed., Text Rev.). Washington, DC: American Psychiatric Association.

Archwamety, T., & Katslyannia, A. (2000). Academic remediation, parole violations, and recidivism rates among delinquent youths. *Remedial and Special Education*, 21, 161–170.

Badian, N. A. (1994). Preschool prediction: Orthographic and phonological skills, and reading. *Annals of Dyslexia*, 44, 3–25.

Badian, N. A. (2000). Do preschool orthographic skills contribute to prediction of reading? In N. A. Badian (Ed.), *Prediction and prevention of reading failure* (pp. 31–56). Timonium, MD: York Press.

Badian, N. A. (2005). Does a visual-orthographic deficit contribute to reading disability. *Annals of Dyslexia*, 55, 28–52.

Bakker, D. J. (1979). Hemispheric difference and reading strategies: Two dyslexias? *Bulletin of the Orton Society*, 29, 84–100.

Bakker, D. J. (2006). Treatment of developmental dyslexia: A review. *Developmental Neurorehabilitation*, 9(1), 3–13.

Bakker, D. J., Licht, R., Kok, A., & Bouma, A. (1980). Cortical responses to word reading by right-and left-eared normal reading-disturbed children. *Journal in Clinical Neuropsychology*, 2, 1–12.

Banks, S. R., Guyer, B. P., & Guyer, K. E. (1993). Spelling improvement by college students with dyslexia, *Annals of Dyslexia*, 43, 186–193.

Bartlett, E. J. (1979). Curriculum, concepts of literacy, and social class. In L. B. Resnick & P. A. Weaver (Eds.). *Theory and practice of early reading* (Vol. 2, pp. 49–72). Hillsdale, NJ: Lawrence Erlbaum Associates.

Beaton, A. A. (2004). *Dyslexia, reading, and the brain: A sourcebook of psychological and biological research*. New York: Psychology Press.

Beck, I. L., Perfetti, C. A., & McKeown, M. G. (1982). Effects of long-term vocabulary instruction on lexical access and reading comprehension. *Journal of Educational Psychology*, 74, 506–521.

Becker, W. C. (1977). Teaching reading and language to the disadvantaged – what we have learned from field research, *Harvard Educational Review*, 47, 518–543.

Bell, N. (1986). *Visualizing and verbalizing for language comprehension and thinking*. Paso Robles, CA: Academy of Reading Publications.

Bell, N. (1991). Gestalt imagery: A critical factor in language comprehension. *Annals of Dyslexia*, 41, 246–260.

Bender, W. M., & Shores, C. (2007). *Response to intervention: A practical guide for every teacher*. Thousand Oaks, CA: Corwin Press.

Berninger, V. W. (1994). *The varieties of orthographic knowledge I: Theoretical and developmental issues*. Dordrecht, Netherlands: Kluwer Academic Publishers.

Berninger, V. W. (1998). *Guides for intervention*. San Antonio, TX: Psychological Corporation.

Berninger, V. W. (2007). *Process Assessment of the Learner: Diagnostics for reading and writing* (2nd ed.). San Antonio, TX: Pearson.

Berninger, V. W., Abbott, R. D., Thompson, J., Wagner, R., Swanson, H. L., Wijsman, E. M., & Raskind, W. (2006). Modeling phonological core deficits within a working memory architecture in children and adults with developmental dyslexia. *Scientific Studies of Reading*, 10, 165–198.

Berninger, V. W., & Graham, S. (1998). Language by hand: A synthesis of a decade of research on handwriting. *Handwriting Review*, 12, 11–25.

Berninger, V. W., & Richards, J. C. (2002). *Brain literacy for educators and psychologists*. San Diego, CA: Academic Press.

Bialystok, E. (2002). Acquisition of literacy in bilingual children: A framework for research. *Language Learning*, 52(1), 159–199.

Bird, J., Bishop, D. V. M., & Freeman, N. H. (1995). Phonological awareness and literacy development in children with expressive phonological impairments. *Journal of Speech and Hearing Research*, 38, 446–462.

Bishop, D. V. M., & Edmundson, A. (1987). Language-impaired 4-year-olds: Distinguishing transient from persistent impairment. *Journal of Speech and Hearing Disorder*, 52, 156–173.

Bishop, D. V. M., & Snowling, M. J. (2004). Developmental dyslexia and specific language impairment: Same or different? *Psychological Bulletin*, 130, 858–886.

Blachman, B. A., Fletcher, J. M., Schatschneider, C., Francis, D. J., Clonan, S. M., Shaywitz, B. A.,& Shaywitz, S. E. (2004). Effects of intensive reading remediation for second and third graders and a 1-year follow-up. *Journal of Educational Psychology*, 96, 444–461.

Blaskey, P., Scheiman, M., Parisis, M., Ciner, E. B., Gallaway, M., & Selznick, R. (1990). The effectiveness of Irlen filters for improving reading performance: A pilot study. *Journal of Learning Disabilities*, 23, 604–612.

Bluestone, C. D., & Klein, J. O. (2001). *Otitis medea in infants and children* (3rd ed.). Philadelphia: Saunders.

Boada, R., Willcutt, E. G., Tunick, R. A., Chhabildas, N. A., Olson, R. K., DeFries, J. C., & Pennington, B. F. (2002). A twin study of the etiology of high reading ability. *Reading and Writing: An Interdisciplinary Journal*, 15, 683–707.

Borman, G. D., Hewes, G. M., Overman, L. T., & Brown, S. (2002). *Comprehensive school reform and student achievement*. Baltimore, MD: Center for Research on the Education of Students Placed at Risk, Johns Hopkins University.

Bowers, P. G. (2001). Exploration of the basis for rapid naming's relationship to reading. In M. Wolfe (Ed.), *Dyslexia, fluency and the brain* (pp. 41–64). Timonium: MD: York Press.

Bowers, P., Sunseth, K., & Golden, J. (1999). The route between rapid naming and reading progress, *Scientific Studies in Reading*, 3, 31–53.

Bowers, P., & Wolf, M. (1993). Theoretical links among naming speed, precise timing mechanisms, and orthographic skill in dyslexia. *Reading and Writing: An Interdisciplinary Journal*, 5, 69–86.

Bradley, L., & Bryant, P. E. (1983). Categorizing sounds and learning to read: A causal connection. *Nature*, 301, 419–421.

Bradley, R., Danielson, L., & Hallahan, D. E. (2002). *Identification of learning disabilities: Research to practice*. Mahwah, NJ: Lawrence Erlbaum.

Brock, S. E., & Christo, C. (2003). Digit naming speed performance among children with attention-deficit/hyperactivity disorder. *The California School Psychologist*, 8, 115–125.

Brock, S. E., Jimerson, S. R., & Hansen, R. L. (2006). *Identifying, assessing, and treating autism at school*. New York: Springer.

Bruce, C., & Salzman, J. A., (2002). Leaving no child behind: Combining project READ and guided reading to improve at-risk students' literacy skills. *Ohio Reading Teacher*, 35, 43–51. Retrieved January 2, 2007, from ProQuest Database.

Bruce, C., Snodgrass, D., & Salzman, J. A. (1999). *A tale of two methods: Melding Project READ and Guided Reading to improve at-risk students' literacy skills*. Paper presented at the Annual Conference of the Mid-Western Educational Research Association, Chicago, IL. (ERIC Document Reproduction Service No. ED 436762).

Burnsman, B. A. (2005). Review of DIBELS: Dynamic Indicators of Basic Early Literacy Skills, Sixth Edition. In R. A. Spies, & B. S. Plake, (Eds.). *The sixteenth mental measurements yearbook*. Lincoln, NE: Buros Institute of Mental Measurements.

Bursuck, W., & Dickson, S. (1999). Implementing a model for preventing reading failure: A report form the field. *Learning Disabilities Research & Practice*, 14, 191–202.

Bush, G. W. (1990, July 17). *Presidential proclamation 6158*. Retrieved December 15, 2007, from http://www.loc.gov/loc/brain/proclaim.html

Buswell, G. T. (1922). *Fundamental reading habits: A study of their development*. Chicago: University of Chicago Press.

Byrne, B., & Fielding-Barnsley, R. (1993). Evaluation of a program to teach phonemic awareness to young children: A 1-year follow-up. *Journal of Educational Psychology*, 85, 104–111.

Byrne, B., Fielding-Barnsley, R., Ashley, L., & Larsen, K. (1997). Assessing the child's and the environment's contribution to reading acquisition: What we know and what we don't know. In B. Blachman (Ed.), *Foundations of reading acquisition and dyslexia: Implications for early intervention* (pp. 265–286). Hillsdale, NJ: Lawrence Erlbaum.

Calfee, R., Lindamood, P., & Lindamood, C. (1973). Acoustic-phonetic skills and reading: Kindergarten through twelve grades. *Journal of Educational Psychology*, 61, 293–298.

Campbell, K. U. (n.d.) *FAQs: Questions about the program*. Retrieved February 24, 2008, from http://www.greatleaps.com/faqs.htm

Campbell, K. U. (1996). *Great Leaps Reading Program*. Gainesville, FL: Diarmuid.

Cardon, L. R., DeFries, J. C., Fulker, D. W., Kimberling, W. J., Pennington, B. F., & Smith, S. D. (1994). Quantitative trait locus for reading disability oh chromosome 6. *Science*, 265, 276–279.

Castles, A., & Coltheart, M. (2004). Is there a causal link from phonological awareness to success in learning to read? *Cognition*, 91, 77–111.

Catts, H. W. (1989). Defining dyslexia as a developmental language disorder. *Annals of Dyslexia*, 39, 50–64.

Catts, H. W. (1993). The relationship between speech-language and reading disabilities. *Journal of Speech and Hearing Research*, 36, 948–958.

Catts, H. W., Adlof, S. M., Hogan, T. P., & Weismer, S. E. (2005). Are specific language impairment and dyslexia distinct disorders? *Journal of Speech, Language & Hearing Research*, 48, 1378–1396.

Catts, H. W., Fey, M. E., Zhang, X., & Tomblin, J. B. (2001). Estimating the risk of future reading difficulties in kindergarten children: A research-based model and its clinical implementation. *Language, Speech & Hearing Services in Schools*, 32, 38–50.

Catts, H. W., & Hogan, T. P. (2003). Language basis of reading disabilities and implications for early identification and remediation. *Reading Psychology*, 24, 223–247.

Catts, H. W., Hogan, T. P., & Fey, M. E. (2003). Subgrouping poor readers on the basis of individual differences in reading-related abilities. *Journal of Learning Disabilities*, 36, 151–165.

Chaban, P. (n.d.). *Irlen filters and learning disabilities*. Retrieved February 23, 2008, from http://www.ldrc.ca/contents/view_article/207/

Chan, L. K., Cole, P. G., & Morris, J. N. (1990). Effects of instruction in the use of a visual-imagery strategy on the reading-comprehension competence of disabled and average readers. *Learning Disability Quarterly*, 13, 2–11.

Christensen, C. A. (2000). Preschool phonological awareness and success in reading. In N. A. Badian (Ed.), *Prediction and prevention of reading failure* (pp. 153–178). Baltimore, MD: York Press.

Cicci, R. (1995). *What's wrong with me: Learning disabilities at home and school*. Timonium, MD: York Press.

Cicci, R. (2001). The gift of dyslexia by Ronald D. Davis. *Perspectives on Language and Literacy*, 27, 10–11.

Cognitive Concepts. (2000). Product overview. Evanston, IL: Antler Earobics.

Coles, G. (2000). *Misreading reading: The bad science that hurts children*. Portsmouth, NH: Heinemann Education Books.

Coltheart, M. (2005). Modeling reading: The dual route approach. In M. J. Snowling & C. Hulme (Eds.), *The science of reading: A handbook* (pp. 6–23). Malden, VA: Blackwell Publishing.

Coordinated Campaign for Learning Disabilities (1997, April). Early warning signs that your child has a learning disability. Retrieved December 17, 2007, from http://www.studentsfirst-tutoring.com/downloads/ccld_early_warning.pdf

Coyne, M. D., & Harn, B. A. (2006). Promoting beginning reading success through meaningful assessment of early literacy skills. *Psychology in the Schools*, 43, 33–43.

Coyne, M. D., Kame'enui, E. J., & Simmons, D. C. (2001). Prevention and intervention in beginning reading: Two complex systems. *Learning Disabilities Research & Practice*, 16, 62–73.

Cunningham, A. E., & Stanovich, K. E. (1990). Assessing print exposure and orthographic processing skill in children: A quick measure of reading experience. *Journal of Educational Psychology*, 82, 733–740.

Cunningham, A. E., & Stanovich, K. E. (1991). Tracking the unique effect of print exposure in children: Associations with vocabulary, general knowledge, and spelling. *Journal of Educational Psychology*, 83, 264–274.

Cunningham, A. E., & Stanovich, K. E. (1993). Children's literacy environments and early word recognition skills. *Reading and Writing: An Interdisciplinary Journal*, 5, 193–204.

Cunningham, A. E., & Stanovich, K. E. (1998). The impact of print exposure on word recognition. In J. Metsala & L. Ehri (Eds.), *Word recognition in beginning literacy* (pp. 235–262). Mahwah, NJ: Erlbaum.

Cunningham, A. E., & Stanovich, K. (1999). What reading does for the mind. *American Educator*, 4, 8–15.

Curran, L., Guin, L., & Marshall, L. (2002). *Improving reading ability through the use of cross age tutuoring: Phono-Graphix and reciprocal teaching*. Master's Thesis, Saint Xavier University. ERIC: ED471073.

Cutting, L., & Denckla, M. (2003). Attention: Relationships between attention deficit hyperactivity disorder and learning disabilities. In H. Swanson, K. Harris, & S. Graham (Eds.), *Handbook of learning disabilities* (pp. 125–139). New York: Guilford Press.

Davis, C., Gayan, J., Knopik, V. S., Smith, S., Cardon, L., Pennington, B., Olson, R., & DeFries, J. (2001). Etiology of reading difficulties and rapid naming: The Colorado Twin Study of Reading Disability. *Behavior Genetics*, 31, 625–635.

Davis, G. N., Lindo, E. J., & Compton, D. L. (2007). Children at risk for reading failure. *Teaching Exceptional Children*, 39, 32–37.

Davis, R. D., & Braun, E. M. (1997). *The gift of dyslexia* (Rev.). New York: The Berkeley Publishing Group.

Davis, R. D., & Braun, E. M. (2003). *The gift of learning*. New York: The Berkeley Publishing Group.

DeFries, J. C., Alarcon, M., & Olson, R. K. (1997). Genetics and dyslexia: Developmental differences in the etiologies of reading and spelling deficits. In C. Hulme & M. Snowling (Eds.), *Dyslexia: Biological bases, identification, & intervention* (pp. 20–37). London: Whurr Publishing.

DeFries, J. C., Falker, D. W., & La Banda, M. C. (1987). Evidence for a genetic aetiology in reading disability of twins. *Nature*, 239, 537–539.

DeFries, J., Olson, R., Pennington, R., & Smith, S. (1991). Colorado reading project: An update. In D. D. Duane & D. B. Gray (Eds.), *The reading brain: The biological basis of dyslexia* (pp. 53–87). Parkton, MD: York Press.

DeFries, J. C., Singer, S. M., Foch, T. T., & Lewitter, F. I. (1978). Familial nature of reading disability. *British Journal of Psychiatry*, 132, 361–367.

deFur, S. (2003). Review of the Test of Early Reading Ability (3rd ed.). In B. S. Plake, J. C. Impara, & R. A. Spies (Eds.). *The fifteenth mental measurements yearbook*. Lincoln, NE: Buros Institute of Mental Measurements.

Deisinger, J. A. (2001). Diagnosis and assessment of autistic spectrum disorders. In T. Wahlberg, F. Obiakor, S. Burkhardt, & A. F. Rotatori (Eds.), *Autistic spectrum disorders: Educational and clinical interventions* (Advances in Special Education, Vol. 14, pp. 181–209). New York: JAI (Elsevier Science).

Denckla, M. B., & Rudel, R. G. (1976a). Naming of pictured objects by dyslexia and other learning disabled children. *Brain and Language*, 3, 1–15.

Denckla, M. B., & Rudel, R. G. (1976b). Rapid "automatized" naming (R.A.N.): Dyslexia differentiated from other learning disabilities. *Neuropsychologia*, 14, 471–479.

Deno, S. L., Fuchs, L. S., Marston, D., & Shin, J. (2001). Using curriculum-based measurement to establish growth standards for students with learning disabilities. *School Psychology Review*, 30, 507–524.

Denton, C. A., Fletcher, J. M., Anthony, J. L., & Francis, D. J. (2006). An evaluation of intensive intervention for students with persistent reading difficulties. *Journal of Learning Disabilities*, 39, 447–466.

Denton, C., & Mathes, P. (2003). Intervention for struggling readers: Possibilities and challenges. In B. Foorman (Ed.), *Preventing and remediating reading difficulties: Bringing science to scale* (pp. 229–252). Baltimore, MD: York Press.

Dickinson, D. K., & Tabors, P. O. (Eds.). (2001). *Building literacy with language: Young children learning at home and school*. Baltimore, MD: Brookes.

Donovan, M. S., & Cross, C. T. (2002). Minority students in special and gifted education. Washington, DC: National Academy Press.

Dore, W., & Rutherford, K. (2001). *Closing the gap*. Paper presented at the BDA 6th International Conference on Dyslexia, York, UK.

Earobics: Helping Readers Reach (n.d.). Retrieved February 23, 2008, from http://www.earobics.com/

Earobics Solutions: Pre-K to 3rd Grade Programs. (n.d.). Retrieved February 24, 2008, from http://www.earobics.com/solutions/programs.php

Eden, G. F., Jones, K. M., Cappell, K., Gareau, L., Wood, F. B., Zeffiro, T. A., Dietz, N. A., Agnew, J. A., & Flowers, D. (2004). Neural changes following remediation in adult developmental dyslexia, *Neuron*, 44, 411–422.

Eden, G., Stein, J., Wood, H., & Wood, F. (1994). Differences in eye movements and reading problems in reading disabled and normal children. *Vision Research*, 34, 1345–1358.

Eden, G., Van Meter, J., Rumsey, J., Maisog, J., Woods, R., & Zeffiro, T. (1996). Abnormal processing of visual motion in dyslexia revealed by functional brain imaging. *Nature*, 382, 66–69.

Eden, G., & Zeffiro, T. (1998). Neural systems affected in developmental dyslexia revealed in functional neuroimaging. *Neuron*, 21, 279–282.

Education for All Handicapped Children Act of 1975, Pub. L. No. 94–142, (1975). Retrieved [summary] February 24, 2008, from http://thomas.loc.gov/cgi-bin/bdquery/z?d094:SN00006:@@@L&summ2=m&

Ehri, L. (1992a). Reconceptualizing the development of sight word reading and in relationship to recoding. In P. B. Gough, L. C. Ehri & R. Treiman (Eds.), *Reading acquisition* (pp. 107–143). Hillsdale NJ: Lawrence Erlbaum.

Ehri, L. (1992b). Review and commentary: Stages of spelling development. In S. Templeton & D. Bear (Eds.), *Development of orthographic knowledge at the foundations of literacy* (pp. 307–332). Hillsdale, NJ: Erlbaum Associates.

Ehri, L. (2000). Learning to read and learning to spell: *Two sides of a coin. Topics in Language Disorders*, 20, 19–36.

Ehri, L. C. (2005). Learning to read words: Theory, findings, and issues. *Scientific Studies of Reading*, 9, 167–188.

Eimas, P. D., & Clarkson, R. L. (1986). Speech perception in children: Are there effects of otitis media? In J. F. Kavanagh (Ed.). *Otitis Media and Child Development*. Parkton, MD: York Press.

Elbro, C., Borstrom, I., & Petersen, D. K. (1998). Predicting dyslexia from kindergarten: The importance of distinctiveness of phonological representations of lexical items. *Reading Research Quarterly*, 33, 36–60.

Enfield, M. L., (1976). An alternate classroom approach to meeting special learning needs of children with reading problems (Doctoral Dissertation, University of Minnesota, 1976). *Digital Dissertations*, DAI-A 37/12, p. 7632, Jun 1977.

Engelmann, S., & Bruner, E. C. (1983). *Reading Mastery I and II: DISTAR Reading*. Chicago, IL: Science Research Associates.

Englemann, S., Carnine, L., & Johnson, G. (1999). *Corrective reading, word attack basics, decoding A*. Columbus, OH: SRA/McGraw-Hill.

Englemann, S., Meyer, L., Johnson, G., & Carnine, L. (1999). Corrective reading, skill applications, decoding C. Columbus, OH: SRA/McGraw-Hill.

Englemann, S., Meyer, L., Carnine, L., Beeker, W., Eisele, J., & Johnson, G. (1999). *Corrective reading, decoding strategies, decoding B1 and B2*. Columbus, OH: SRA/McGraw-Hill.

Evans, B. J. W. (1999). Do visual problems cause dyslexia? *Ophthalmic Physiological Optics*, 19, 277–278.

Fawcett, A. J., & Nicolson, R. I. (2000). Systemic screening and intervention for reading difficulty. In N. A. Badian (Ed.), *Prediction and prevention of reading failure* (pp. 57–86). Baltimore, MD: York Press.

Fawcett, A. J., Nicolson, R., & Lee, R. (2004). *Ready to learn*. San Antonio, TX: Harcourt Assessment.

Feifer, S., & De Fina, P. (2000). *The neuropsychology of reading disorders: Diagnosis and intervention workbook*. Middleton MD: School Neuropsych Press.

Felton, R. H. (1992). Early identification of children at risk for reading disabilities. *Topics in Early Childhood Special Education*, 12, 212–229.

Felton, R. H., & Brown, I. S. (1990). Phonological processes as predictors of specific reading skills in children at risk for reading failure. *Reading and Writing*, 2, 39–59.

Felton, R., Wood, F., Brown, I., Campbell, S., & Harter, M. (1987). Separate verbal memory and naming deficits in attention deficit disorder and reading disability. *Brain and Language*, 31, 171–184.

Fenton, R. (2005). Review of the Test of Phonological Awareness-Second Edition: PLUS. In R. A. Spies & B. S. Plake, (Eds.). *The sixteenth mental measurements yearbook*. Lincoln, NE: Buros Institute of Mental Measurements.

Fernald, G. M., & Keller, H. (1921). The effect of kinesthetic factors in development of word recognition in the case of non-readers. *Journal of Educational Research*, 4, 355–377.

Fill, M., Gips, M., & Hosty, K. (1998). The Phono-Graphix method for teaching reading and spelling. *The Clinical Connection*, 11, 4.

Finn, C., Rotherman, A., & Hokanson, C. E. (2001). *Rethinking special education for a new century*. Washington, DC: Thomas B. Fordham Foundation and Progressive Policy Institute.

Finn, J. D., Stott, & Zarichny, K. T. (1988). School performance and adolescents in juvenile court. *Urban Education*, 23, 151–162.

Fisher, S. E., & DeFries, J. C. (2002). Developmental dyslexia: Genetic dissection of a complex cognitive trait. *Natural Reviews Neuroscience*, 3, 767–780.

Flanagan, D., & Ortiz, S. (2001). *Essentials of cross battery assessment*. New York: Wiley.

Flanagan, D. P., Ortiz, S. O., & Alfonso, V. C. (2007). Essentials of cross battery assessment: Second edition. New York: Wiley.

Flanagan, D. P., Ortiz, S. O., Alfonso, V. C., & Dynda, A. M. (2006). Integration of response to intervention and norm-referenced tests in learning disability identification: Learning from the Tower of Babel. *Psychology in the Schools*, 43, 807–825.

Flanagan, D. P., Ortiz, S. O., Alfonso, V. C., & Mascolo, J. T. (2002). *The achievement test desk reference (ATDR): Comprehensive assessment and learning disabilities*. Boston: Allyn & Bacon.

Flanagan, D. P., Ortiz, S. O., Alfonso, V. C., & Mascolo, J. T. (2006). *The achievement test desk reference: A guide to learning disabilities identification* (2nd ed.). Hoboken, NJ: Wiley.

Fletcher, J. M. (2005). Predicting math outcomes: Reading predictors and comorbidity. *Journal of Learning Disabilities*, 38, 308–312.

Fletcher, J. M., Foorman, B. R., Shaywitz, S. E., & Shaywitz, B. (1999). Conceptual and methodological issues in dyslexia research: A lesson for developmental disorders. In H. Tager-Flugsberg (Ed.), *Neurodevelopmental disorders* (pp. 271–306). Cambridge, MA: MIT Press.

Fletcher, J. M., Lyon, G. R., Fuchs, L. S., & Barnes, M. A. (2007). *Learning disabilities: From identification to intervention*. New York: Guilford Press.

Fletcher, J. M., & Shaywitz, S. E. (1994). Cognitive profiles of reading disability: Comparisons of discrepancy and low achievement. *Journal of Educational Psychology*, 86, 6–23.

Flynn, J. M., & Childs, B. (1994). Prevalence of reading failure in boys compared with girls. *Psychology in the Schools*, 31, 66–71.

Flynn, J. M., & Rahbar M. H. (1994). Prevalence of reading failure in boys compared with girls. *Psychology in the Schools*, 31, 66–71.

Foorman, B. R. (2003). *Preventing and remediating reading difficulties: Bringing science to scale*. Baltimore, MD: York Press.

Foorman, B. R., Breier, J. I., & Fletcher, J. M. (2003). Interventions aimed at improving reading success: An evidence-based approach. *Developmental Neuropsychology*, 24, 613–640.

Foorman, B. R., Francis, D. J., Fletcher, P., Schwartz, J., & Mehta, P. (1998). The role of instruction in learning to read: Preventing reading failure in at-risk children. *Journal of Educational Psychology*, 90, 37–55.

Foorman, B. R., Francis, D. J., & Shaywitz, S. E. (1997). The case for early intervention. In B. Blachman (Ed.), *Foundations of reading acquisition and dyslexia* (pp. 243–264). Mahwah, NJ: Lawrence Erlbaum.

Frieden, L. (2004). *Improving outcomes for students with disabilities*. Washington, DC: National Council on Disabilities.

Fuchs, D., Fuchs, L. S., & Compton, D. L. (2004). Identifying reading disabilities by responsiveness-to-instruction: Specifying measures and criteria. *Learning Disability Quarterly, 27*(4), 216–227.

Fuchs, L. (2003). Assessing intervention responsiveness: Conceptual and technical issues. *Learning Disabilities Research and Practice, 18*(3), 172–186.

Fuchs, L. S. (2004). The past, present, and future of curriculum-based measurement research. *School Psychology Review, 33*(2), 188–192.

Fuchs, L. S., & Fuchs, D. (2006). Implementing responsiveness to intervention to identify learning disabilities. *Perspectives on Dyslexia, 32*, 39–43.

Fuchs, L., Fuchs, D., & Compton, D. (2004). Monitoring early reading development in first graders: Word identification fluency versus nonsense word fluency. *Exceptional Children, 1*, 7–21.

Fuchs, D., Fuchs, L. S., & Compton, D. L. (2004). Identifying reading disabilities by responsiveness-to-instruction: Specifying measures and criteria. *Learning Disability Quarterly, 27*(4), 216–227.

Fuchs, L. S., Fuchs, P., Hosp, M. K., & Jenkins, J. R. (2001). Oral reading fluency as an indicator of reading competence: A theoretical, empirical, and historical analysis. *Scientific Studies of Reading, 5*, 239–256.

Fuchs, L. S., Fuchs, D., & Maxwell, L. (1988). The validity of informal reading comprehension measures. *Remedial and Special Education, 9*, 20–28.

Gaab, N., Gabrielli, J. D., Deutsch, G. K., Tallal, P., & Temple, E. (2007). Neural correlates of rapid auditory processing are disrupted in children with developmental dyslexia and ameliorated with training: An fMRI study. *Restorative Neurology and Neuroscience, 25*, 295–310.

Ganshow, L., & Miles, T. (2000). Dyslexia across the world. *Perspectives, 26*, 12–35.

Gayan, J., & Olson, R. (2005). Genetic and environmental influences on orthographic and phonological skills in children with reading disabilities. *Developmental Neuropsychology, 20*, 487–511.

Gersten, R., & Baker, S. (2001). Teaching expressive writing to students with learning disabilities: A meta-analysis. *The Elementary School Journal, 101*, 251–272.

Gersten, R., Baker, S. K., Shanahan, T., Linan-Thompson, S., Collins, P., & Scarcella, R. (2007). Effective Literacy and English Language Instruction for English Learners in the Elementary Grades: A Practice Guide (NCEE 2007–4011). Washington, DC: National Center for Education Evaluation and Regional Assistance, Institute of Education Sciences, U.S. Department of Education. Retrieved from http://ies.ed.gov/ncee.

Gersten, R., Darch, C., & Gleason, M. (1988). Effectiveness of a direct instruction academic kindergarten for low income students. *The Elementary School Journal, 89*, 227–240.

Gersten, R., Woodward, J., & Darch, C. (1986). Direct instruction: A research-based approach to curriculum design and teaching. *Exceptional Children, 53*, 17–31.

Geva, E. (2000). Issues in the assessment of reading disabilities in L2 children: Beliefs and research evidence. *Dyslexia, 6*(1), 13–28.

Geva, E., Yaghoub-Zadeh, Z., Schuster, B. (2000). Understanding individual differences in word recognition skills of ESL children. *Annals of Dyslexia, 50*, 123–154.

Gijsel, M. A., Bosman, A. M. T., & Verhoeven, L. (2006). Kindergarten risk factors, cognitive factors, and teacher judgments as predictors of early reading in Dutch. *Journal of Learning Disabilities, 39*, 558–571.

Gillingham, A., & Stillman, B. (1960). *Remedial training for children with specific disability in reading*. Cambridge, MA: Educators Publishing Service.

Gillingham, A., & Stillman, B. (1970). *Remedial training for children with specific difficulty in reading, spelling, and penmanship*. Cambridge, MA: Educators Publishing Service.

Gilmor, T. (1999). The efficacy of the Tomatis Method for children with learning and communication disorders: A meta-analysis. *International Journal of Listening, 13*, 12–23.

Goin, R. P., & Myers, B. J. (2004). Characteristics of infantile autism: Moving towards earlier detection. *Focus on Autism and Other Developmental Disabilities, 19*, 5–12.

Goldberg, R. J., Higgins, E. L., Raskind, M. H., & Herman, K. L. (2003). Predictors of success in individuals with learning disabilities: A qualitative analysis of a 20-year longitudinal study. *Learning Disabilities Research & Practice*, 18, 222–236.

Good, R. H., Kaminski, R. A., Moats, L. C., Laimon, D., Smith, S., & Dill, S. (2003). *DIBELS: Dynamic Indicators of Basic Early Literacy Skills* (6th ed.). Longmont, CO: Sopris West.

Good, R. H., Simmons, D. C., & Kame'enui, E. J. (2001). The importance and decision-making utility of a continuum of fluency-based indicators of foundational reading skills for third-grade high-stakes outcomes. *Scientific Studies of Reading*, 5, 257–288.

Goswami, U. (2000). Phonological representations, reading development and dyslexia: Towards a cross-linguistic theoretical framework. *Dyslexia*, 6, 133–151.

Goswani, U. (2001). Early phonological development and the acquisition of literacy. In S. Neumann & D. K. Dickinson (Eds.), *Handbook of early literacy research* (pp. 111–125). New York: Guilford Press.

Goswami, U. (2005). Synthetic phonics and learning to read: A cross-language perspective. *Educational Psychology in Practice*, 21, 273–282.

Gottardo, A. (2002). The relationship between language and reading skills in bilingual Spanish-English speakers. *Topics in Language Disorders*, 22(5), 46–70.

Gough, P. B., & Tunmer, W. E. (1986). Decoding, reading and reading disability. *Remedial & Special Education*, 7, 6–10.

Gredler, G. R. (2000). Early childhood screening for developmental and educational problems. In B. A. Bracken (Ed.), *The psychoeducational assessment of preschool children* (pp. 399–411). Boston: Allyn & Bacon.

Greene, J. F. (1996). LANGUAGE! Effects of an individualized structured language curriculum for middle and high school students. *Annals of Dyslexia*, 46, 97–121.

Gregory, R. P., Hackney, C., & Gregory, N. M. (1982). Corrective reading programme: An evaluation. *British Journal of Educational Psychology*, 52, 33–50.

Grigorencko, E. L., Wood, F. B., Meyer, M. S., Hart, L. A., Speed, W. C., Shuster, A., & D. Pauls. (1997). Susceptibility loci for distinct components of developmental dyslexia on chromosome 6 and 15. *American Journal of Human Genetics*, 60, 27–39.

Hale, J. B., & Fiorello, C. A. (2004). *School neuropsychology: A practitioner's handbook*. NY: Guilford Press.

Hall, S. L. (2006). *I've DIBEL'd, now what?: Designing interventions with DIBELS data*. Longmont, CO: Sopris West.

Hallahan, D. P., & Kauffman, J. M. (2000). *Exceptional learners: Introduction to special educations* (8th ed.). Boston: Allyn & Bacon.

Hallgren, B. (1950). Specific dyslexia (congenital word-blindness): A clinical and genetic study. *Acta Psychiatrica et Neurologica Supplement*, 65, 1–287.

Hammill, D. D. (2004). What we know about correlates of reading. *Exceptional Children*, 70, 453–468.

Hammill, D. D., Mather, N., Allen, E. A., & Roberts, R. (2002). Using semantics, grammar, phonology, and rapid naming tasks to predict word identification. *Journal of Learning Disabilities*, 35, 121–137.

Hammill, D. D., & Newcomber, P. L. (1997). *Test of Language Development-Intermediate* (3rd ed.). Austin, TX: Pro-Ed.

Hanley, J. R. (2005). Learning to read in Chinese. In M. J. Snowling & C. Hulme (Eds.), *The science of reading: A handbook* (pp. 316–334). Malden, MA: Blackwell Publishers.

Hasbrouck, J. E., & Tindal, G. (1992). Curriculum-based oral reading fluency norms for students in grades 2 through 5. *Teaching Exceptional Children*, 24, 41–44.

Hintze, J. M., Ryan, A. L., & Stoner, G. (2003). Concurrent validity and diagnostic accuracy of the Dynamic Indicators of Basic Early Literacy Skills and the Comprehensive Test of Phonological Processing. *School Psychology Review*, 32, 541–556.

Hoeft, F., Hernandez, A., McMillon, G., Taylor-Hill, H., Martindale, J. L., Meyler, A., Keller, T. A., Ting Siok, W., Deutsch, G. K., Just, M. A., Whitfield-Gabrieli, S., & Gabrieli, J. D. E. (2006). Neural basis of dyslexia: A comparison between dyslexic and nondyslexic children equated for reading ability. *Journal of Neuroscience*, 26, 10700–10708.

Hook, P. E., Macaruso, P., & Jones, S. (2001). Efficacy of Fast ForWord training on facilitating acquisition of reading skills by children with reading difficulties – A longitudinal study. *Annals of Dyslexia*, 51, 75–96.

Howell, K. W., & Nolet, V. (2000). Curriculum based evaluation for special and remedial education (3rd ed.). Atlanta, GA: Wadsworth.

Huff, E. G., Dancer, J., Evans, S. D., & Skoch, A. C. (2006). Validity and reliability of the Test of Early Reading Ability-Second Edition with preschool age children. *Perceptual & Motor Skills*, 102, 288–290.

Individuals with Disabilities Eduction Improvement Act of 2004, Pub. L. No. 108–446, (2004). Retrieved [summary] February 23, 2008, from http://thomas.loc.gov/cgi-bin/bdquery/z?d108: HR01350:@@@L&summ2=m&

International Dyslexia Association, News Release, October 23, 2004. Also published on Mental Health Watch, http://www.mentalhealthwatch.org/reports/dore.shtml.

International Dyslexia Association, (2007). *Dyslexia basics fact sheet – 8/07*. Retrieved September 30, 2007, from http://www.interdys.org/ewebeditpro5/upload/Dyslexia_Basics_FS_-_final_81407.pdf

Irlen, H. (1983). *Successful treatment of learning disabilities*. Paper presented at the 91st Annual Convention of the American Psychological Association, Anaheim, CA.

Irlen, H. (2005). *Reading by the colors: Overcoming dyslexia and other reading disabilities through the Irlen Method* (Rev.). New York: Perigree.

Isaacson, S. L. (1996). Simple ways to assess the writing skills of students with learning disabilities. *The Volta Review*, 98, 183–199.

Jimerson, S. R., Burns, M. K., & VanDerHeyden, A. M. (Eds) (2007). *Handbook of response to intervention: The science and practice of assessment and intervention*. New York: Springer.

Johnson, B. (2005). Psychological comorbidity in children and adolescents with learning disorders. *Journal of Indian Association for Child and Adolescent Mental Health*, 1(1), Article 7.

Johnson, D. J., & Myklebust, H. (1967). *Learning disabilities: Educational principles and practices*. New York: Grune & Stratton.

Johnson-Glenberg, M. C. (2000). Training reading comprehension in adequate decoders/poor comprehenders: Verbal versus visual strategies. *Journal of Educational Psychology*, 92, 772–782.

Juel, C., & Leavell, J. A. (1988). Retention and nonretention of at-risk readers in first grade and their subsequent reaching achievement. *Journal of Learning Disabilities*, 21, 572–582.

Kame'enui, E. J., Simmons, D. C., Good, R. J., & Harn, B. A. (2001). The use of fluency based measures in early identification and evaluation of intervention efficacy in schools. In M. Wolfe (Ed.), *Dyslexia, fluency and the brain* (pp. 307–332). Timonium, MD: York Press.

Kamenski, R., & Good, R. J. (1996). Toward a technology for assessing basic early literacy skills. *School Psychology Review*, 25, 215–227.

Kaufman, A. S., & Kaufman, N. (2004). *Kaufman Test of Educational Achievement-Second Edition, Comprehensive Form*. Bloomington, MN: Pearson.

Kavale, K. A., & Forness, S. R. (2000). What definitions of learning disabilities say and don't say: A critical analysis. *Journal of Learning Disabilities*, 33(3), 239–256.

Kavale, K. A., & Reese, L. (1992). The character of learning disabilities: An Iowa profile. *Learning Disabilities Quarterly*, 15, 74–94.

Kennedy, K., & Brackman, J. (1993). Effectiveness of the Lindamood Auditory Discrimination in Depth Program for students with learning disabilities. *Learning Disabilities Research and Practice*, 8, 253–259.

Kershner, J., Cummings, R., Clarke, K., Hadfield, A., & Kershner, B. (1986). Evaluation of the Tomatis Listening Training Program with learning disabled children. *Canadian Journal of Special Education*, 2, 1–32.

Kershner, J., Cummings, R., Clarke, K., Hadfield, A., & Kershner, B. (1990). Two-year evaluation of the Tomatis Listneing Training Program with learning disabled children. *Learning Disability Quarterly*, 13, 43–53.

Keys, M. (2001). Optometric visual training. *Perspectives on Language and Literacy*, 27, 14–15.

Kirk, S. A., & Elkins, J. (1975). Characteristics of children enrolled in Child Service Demonstration Centers. *Journal of Learning Disabilities*, 8, 630–637.

Korkman, M., Kirk, U., & Kemp, S. (2007). NEPSY: A developmental neuropsychological assessment (2nd ed.). San Antonia, TX: Psychological Corporation/Harcourt & Brace.

Lachmann, T. (2002). Reading disability as a deficit in functional coordination. In E. Witruk, A. D. Friederici, & T. Lachmann (Eds.), *Basic functions of language, reading, and reading disability* (pp. 165–198). Boston: Kluwer Academic Publishers.

Lajiness-O'Neill[AU2] Please update Lajiness-O'Neill et al. (in press)., R., Akamine, Y., & Bowyer, S. Treatment effects of Fast ForWord demonstrated by magnetoencephalography (MEG) in a child with developmental dyslexia. *Neurocase* (in press).

Lee, J., Grigg, W., & Donahue, P. (2007). *The nation's report card 2007 (NCES 2007–496)*. Washington, DC: National Center on Educational Progress.

Leppanen, P. H. T., & Lyytinen, H. (1997). Auditory event-related potentials in the study of developmental language related disorders. *Audiology & Neurology*, 2, 308–340 and EXP.

Lerner, J. (2003). *Learning disabilities: Theories, diagnosis, and teaching strategies*. New York: Houghton Mifflin.

Liberman, A. M. (1999). The reading researcher and the reading teacher need the right theory of speech. *Scientific Studies of Reading*, 3, 95.

Liberman, I. Y., & Shankweiler, D. (1985). Phonology and problems of learning to read and write. *Remedial and Special Education*, 6, 8–17.

Liberman, I. Y., Shankweiler, D., & Liberman, A. M. (1989). The alphabetic principle and learning to read. In A. M. Liberman & D. Shankweiler (Eds.), *Phonology and reading disabiity: Solving the reading puzzle* (pp. 1–34). Ann Arbor: University of Michigan Press.

Liberman, I. Y., Shankweiler, D., Liberman, A. M., Fowler, C., & Fisher, F. W. (1977). Phonetic segmentation and recoding in the beginning reader. In A. S. Rober & D. L. Scarborough (Eds.), *Toward a psychology of reading* (pp. 207–225). Hillsdale, NJ: Lawrence Erlbaum.

Lieberman, I. Y., Shankweiler, D. P., Orlando, C., Harris, K., & Bell-Beitz, F. (1971). Letter confusions and reversals of sequence in the beginning reader: Implications for Orton's theory of developmental dyslexia. *Cortex*, 7, 127–142.

Liederman, J., Kantrowitz, L., & Flannery, K. (2005). Male vulnerability to reading disability is not likely to be a myth: A call for new data. *Journal of Learning Disabilities*, 38, 109–129.

Lindamood, P., & Lindamood, P. (1998). *Lindamood phonemic sequencing (LiPS) program*. Austin, TX: Pro-Ed.

Lockavitch, J. (1996). *Failure free reading*. Concord, NC: Failure Free Reading.

Lovett, M., Steinback, K., & Fritjers, J. (2000). Remediating the core deficits of developmental reading disability: A double deficit perspective. *Journal of Learning Disabilities*, 33, 334–359.

Lubs, H., Rabin, M., Feldman, E., Jallad, B., Kushc, A., & Gross-Glenn, K. (1993). Familial dyslexia: Genetic and medical findings in eleven three generation families. *Annals of Dyslexia*, 43, 44–60.

Lyon, G. R. (1995). Toward a definition of dyslexia. *Annals of Dyslexia*, 45, 3–27.

Lyon, G. R., Fletcher, J. M., Shaywitz, B., Shaywitz, S. E., Torgesen, J. K., Wood, F. B., Shulte, A., & Olson, R. (2001). Rethinking learning disabilities. In C. R. Hokanson (Ed.), *Rethinking special education for a new century* (pp. 259–287). Washington, DC: Thomas B. Fordham Foundation and Progressive Policy Institute.

Lyon, G. R., & Moats, L. C. (1997). Critical conceptual and methodological considerations in reading intervention research. *Journal of Learning Disabilities*, 30, 578–588.

Lyon, G. R., Shaywitz, S. E., & Shaywitz, B. A. (2003). Defining dyslexia, comorbidity, teachers' knowledge of language and reading: A definition of dyslexia. *Annals of Dyslexia*, 53, 1–14.

Lyytinen, H., Aro, M., Eklund, K., Erskine, J., Guttorm, T., Laakso, M., Leppanen, P., Lyytinen, P., Poieus, A., Richardson, U., & Torppa, M. (2004). The development of children at familial risk for dyslexia: Birth to early school age. *Annals of Dyslexia*, 54, 178–183.

MacPhee, K. (1990). *Spell read phonological auditory training (P.A.T.)*. Rockville, MD: P.A.T. Learning Systems.

Madden, N. A. (1995). *Reading Roots: Teachers' manual*. Baltimore, MD: Center for Research on Effective Schooling for Disadvantaged Students, Johns Hopkins University.

Madden, N. A., Slavin, R. E., Farnish, A. M., Livingston, M. A., Calderon, M., & Steven, R. J. (1996). *Reading Wings: Teachers' manual*. Baltimore, MD: Center for Research on Effective Schooling for Disadvantaged Students, Johns Hopkins University.

Madden, N. A., Slavin, R. E., Karweit, N. L., Dolan, L. J., & Wasik, B. A. (1993). Success for All: Longitudinal effects of a restructuring program for inner-city elementary schools. *American Educational Research Journal, 30*, 123–148.

Madden, N. A., Wasik, B. A., & Petza, R. (1989). *Writing from the heart: A writing process approach for first and second graders*. Baltimore, MD: Center for Research on Effective Schooling for Disadvantaged Students, Johns Hopkins University.

Manis, F. R., Doi, L. M., & Bhada, B. (2000). Naming speed, phonological awareness, and orthographic knowledge in second graders. *Journal of Learning Disabilities, 33*, 325–333.

Manis, F. R., & Freedman, L. (2001). The relationship of naming speed to multiple reading measures in disabled and normal readers. In M. Wolf (Ed.), *Dyslexia, fluency and the brain* (pp. 65–92). Timonium, MD: York Press.

Manis, F. R., Seidenberg, M. S., & Doi, L. M. (1999). See Dick RAN: Rapid naming and the longitudinal prediction of reading subskills in first and second graders. *Scientific Studies of Reading, 3*, 129–157.

Mann, V., & Lieberman, I. Y. (1984). Phonological awareness and verbal short term memory. *Journal of Learning Disabilities, 17*, 592–599.

Marrs, H. & Patrick, C. (2002). A return to eye-movement training? An evaluation of the reading plus program. Reading Psychology, 23, 297–322.

Mathes, P. G., Denton, C. A., Fletcher, P., Anthony, J. L., Francis, D. J., & Schatschneider, C. (2005). An evaluation of two reading interventions derived from diverse models. *Reading Research Quarterly, 40*, 148–183.

McArthur, Hogben, G. M., Edwards, V. T., Health, S. M., & Mengler, E. D. (2000). On the "specifics" of specific reading disability and specific language impairment. *Journal of Child Psychology and Psychiatry, 41*, 869–874.

McCabe, R. (2002). *The efficacy of Lexia skills based software for improving reading comprehension*. Lincoln, MA: Lexia.

McCardle, P., Scarborough, H. S., & Catts, H. W. (2001). Predicting, explaining, and preventing children's reading difficulties. *Learning Disabilities Research & Practice, 16*, 230–239.

McGuinness, C., & McGuinness, G. (1999). *Reading reflex*. New York: Fireside.

McGuinness, C., McGuinness, D., & McGuinness, G. (1996). Phono-Graphix: A new method for remediation reading difficulties. *Annals of Dyslexia, 46*, 73–96.

McMaster, K. L., Fuchs, D., Fuchs, L. S., & Compton, D. L. (2005). Responding to nonresponders: An experimental field trial of identification and intervention methods. *Exceptional Children, 71*, 445–463.

McNamara, J. K., Scissons, M., & Dahleu, J. (2005). A longitudinal study of early identification markers for children at-risk for reading disabilities: The Matthew effect and the challenge of over-identification. *Reading Improvement, 42*, 80–97.

McRae, D. J. (2002). *Test score gains for Open Court schools in California: Results from three cohorts of schools*. Columbus, OH: SRA/McGraw-Hill. Retrieved February 24, 2008, from https://www.sraonline.com/download/OCR/Research/testscoresgain.pdf

Mellard, D. F., & Johnson, E. (2008). *RTI: A practitioner's guide to implementing response to intervention*. Thousand Oaks, CA: Corwin Press.

Mellard, D., & Woods, S. (2007). Adult life with dyslexia. *Perspectives, 33*(4), 15–18.

Menyuk, P. (1986). Predicting speech and language problems with persistent otitis medea. In J. F. Kavanagh (Ed.), *Otitis medea and child development*. Parkton, MD: York Press.

Mercer, C. D., Campbell, K. N., Miller, W. D., Mercer, K. D., & Lane, H. B. (2002). Effects of a reading fluency intervention for middle schoolers with specific learning disabilities. *Learning Disabilities Research and Practice, 15*, 179–189.

Merzenich, M. M., Jenkins, W. M., Johnson, P., Scheiner, C., Miller, S. C., & Tallal, P. (1996). Temporal processing deficits of language-learning in paired children ameliorated by training. *Science*, 271, 77–81.

Meyer, L. A., Gersten, R. M., & Gutkin, J. (1983). Direct instruction: A project follow-through success story in an inner-city school. *Elementary School Journal*, 84, 241–252.

Meyer, M., & Felton, R. (1999). Repeated reading to enhance fluency: Old approaches and new directions. *Annals of Dyslexia*, 49, 283–306.

Miles, T. R. (2004). Some problems in determining the prevalence of dyslexia. *Electronic Journal of Research in Educational Psychology*, 2, 5–12.

Miller, S., & Tallel, P. (1996). Acoustically modified speech training studies: Implications for dyslexia? *Perspectives: Proceedings of the Orton Dyslexia Society*, 22, 8–9.

Moats, L. C. (1999). *Basic facts about dyslexia part II: What every professional ought to know.* Baltimore, MD: International Dyslexia Association.

Moats, L. (2000). *Speech to print: Language essentials for teachers.* Baltimore, MD: Brooks.

Mody, M., Schwartz, R. G., Gravel, G. S., & Ruben, R. J. (1999). Speech perception and verbal meaning in children with and without histories of otitis medea. *Journal of Speech, Language and Hearing Research*, 42, 1069–1079.

Molfese, P. L. (2000). Predicting dyslexia at 8 years of age using neonatal brain responses. *Brain and Language*, 72, 238–245.

Molfese, V., Molfese, D., & Modglin, A. (2001). Newborn and preschool predictors of second-grade reading scores: An evaluation of categorical and continuous scores. *Journal of Learning Disabilities*, 34, 545–554.

Morgan, P. L., & Sideridis, G. D. (2006). Contrasting the effectiveness of fluency interventions for students with or at risk for learning disabilities: a multi-level random coefficient modeling meta-analysis. *Learning Disabilities Research*, 21, 191–210.

Morgan, W. P. (1896). A case of congenital word blindness. *The British Medical Journal*, 2, 1378.

Morris, R. D., & Shaywitz, S. E. (1998). Subtypes of reading disability: Variability around a phonological core. *Journal of Educational Psychology*, 90, 347–374.

Moustafa, M., & Land, R. E. (2002). The reading achievement of economically-disadvantaged children in urban schools using *Open Court* vs. comparably disadvantaged children in urban schools using non-scripted reading programs. *2002 Yearbook of the Urban Learning, Teaching, and Research Special Interest Group of the American Educational Research Association* (pp. 44–53). Retrieved February 23, 2008, from http://instructional1.calstatela.edu/mmousta/The_Reading_Achievement_of_Economically_Disadvantaged_Children_in_Urban_Schools_Using_Open_Court.htm

Muter, V. (1994). Influence of phonological awareness and letter knowledge on beginning reading and spelling development. In C. Hulme & M. J. Snowling (Eds.), *Reading development and dyslexia* (pp. 45–62). San Diego, CA: Singular.

Muter, V. (2000). Screening for early reading failure. In N. A. Badian (Ed.), *Prediction and prevention of reading failure* (pp. 1–30). Timonium, MD: York Press.

Muter, V., Hulme, C., & Snowling, M. (1997). *Phonological Abilities Test.* Minneapolis, MN: Pearson Assessment.

Muter, V., & Snowling, M. J. (1998). Concurrent and longitudinal predictors of reading: The role of metalinguistic and short-term memory skills. *Reading Research Quarterly*, 33, 320–337.

Nathan, L., Stackhouse, J., Goulandris, N., & Snowling, M. J. (2004). Educational consequences of developmental speech disorder: Key Stage I National Curriculum assessment results in English and mathematics. *British Journal of Educational Psychology*, 74, 173–186.

Nation, K., & Hulme, C. (1997). Phonemic segmentation, not onset-rime segmentation, predicts early reading and spelling skills. *Reading Research Quarterly*, 32, 154–167.

National Association of State Directors of Special Education. (2007). *Response to intervention; Policy considerations and implementation.* Arlington, VA: Author.

National Center for Education Statistics (1998). *National Assessment of Educational Progress.* Retrieved January 30, 2008 from http://nces.ed.gov/nationalreportcard/pubs/main1998/1999462.ntml

National Endowment for the Arts. (2004). *Reading at risk: A survey of literary reading in America* (Research report No. # 46). Washington, DC: Author.

National Institute for Child Health and Human Development. (1999). Keys to successful learning (pp. 1–3). Washington, DC: Author.

National Institute of Child Health & Development. (2007). *Learning disabilities: What are learning disabilities?* Retrieved December 15, 2007, from http://www.nichd.nih.gov/health/topics/learning_disabilities.cfm

National Institute on Deafness and Other Communication Disorders (2004). *Auditory processing disorder in children.* Retrieved January 30, 2008, from http://www.ldonline.org/article/8056

National Reading Panel. (2000). *Report of the national reading panel: Teaching children to read: An evidence-based assessment of the scientific research literature and its implications for reading instruction* (Publication No. 00-4754). Rockville, MD: NICHD Clearinghouse.

Newcomber, P. L., & Hammill, D. D. (1997). *Test of Language Development-Primary* (3rd ed.). Austin, TX: Pro-Ed.

Nicolson, R., & Fawcett, A. (2004). *Dyslexia Screening Test- Junior.* San Antonio, TX: The Psychological Corporation.

Nicolson, R. I., Fawcett, A. J., & Dean, P. (2001). Developmental dyslexia: The cerebellar deficit hypothesis. *Trends in Neurosciences*, 24, 508–511.

Nittrouer, S. (1995). The relation between speech perception and phonemic awareness: Evidence from Low S.E.S. children and children with chronic otitis medea. *Journal of Speech and Hearing Research*, 39, 1059–1070.

No Child Left Behind Act of 2001, Pub. L. No. 107–110, § 1208(3) (2002). Retrieved February 23, 2008, from http://www.ed.gov/policy/elsec/leg/esea02/index.html

O'Brien, N., Langhinrichsen-Rohling, J., & Shelley-Tremblay, J. (2007). Reading problems, attentional deficits, and current mental health status in adjudicated adolescent males. *Journal of Correctional Education*, 12, 376–392.

O'Connor, P. D., Sofo, F., Kendall, L., & Olsen, G. (1990). Reading disabilities and the effects of colored filters. *Journal of Learning Disabilities*, 23, 613–620.

O'Connor, R. E., Fulmer, D., Harty, K. R., & Bell, K. M. (2005). Layers of reading intervention in kindergarten through third grade: Changes in teaching and student outcomes. *Journal of Learning Disabilities*, 38, 440–455.

O'Connor, R. E., & Jenkins, J. R. (1999). Prediction of reading disabilities in kindergarten and first grade. *Scientific Studies of Reading*, 3, 159–197.

O'Connor, J. and Wilson, B. 1995. *Effectiveness of the Wilson Reading System® used in public school training.* In McIntyre, C., and Pickering, J. (eds). Clinical studies of Multisensory Structured Language Education. Salem, OR: International Multisensory Structured Language Education Council.

Olson, R. K., Forsberg, H., & Wise, B. (1994). Genes, environment, and the development of orthographic skills. In V. W. Berninger (Ed.), *The varieties of orthographic knowledge I: Theoretical and developmental issues* (pp. 27–71). Dordrecht, Netherlands: Kluwer Academic Publishers.

Open Court Reading, California 2002 Edition. (2002). Columbus, OH: SRA/McGraw Hill.

Orton, J. (1976). *A guide to teaching phonics.* Cambridge, MA: Educators Publishing Service.

Orton, S. (1928). Specific reading disability- strephosymbolia. *Journal of the American Medical Association*, 90, 1095–1099.

Palombo, J. (2001). Learning disorders and disorders of the self in children and adolescents. New York: Northam.

Parker, R. M. (1990). Power, control, and validity in research. *Journal of Learning Disabilities*, 23, 613–620.

Pauc, R. (2005). Comorbidity of dyslexia, dyspraxia, attention deficit disorder (ADD), attention deficit hyperactive disorder (AD/HD), obsessive compulsive disorder and Tourette's syndrome in children: A prospective epidemiological study. *Clinical Chiropractic*, 8, 189–198.

Pennington, B. F., Bender, B., Puck, M., Salbenblatt, J., & Robinson, A. (1982). Learning disabilities in children with sex chromosome anomalies. *Child Development*, 53, 1182–1192.

Pennington, B. F., Gilger, J., Pauls, D., Smith, S. A., Smith, S. D., & DeFries, J. C. (1991). Evidence for major gene transmission of developmental dyslexia. *Journal of the American Medical Association*, 266, 1527–1534.

Pennington, B. F., & Lefly, D. L. (2001). Early reading development in children at family risk for dyslexia. *Child Development*, 72, 816–833.

Pennington, B. F., & Olson, R. K. (2005). Genetics of dyslexia. In M. J. Snowling & C. Hulme (Eds.), *The science of reading: A handbook* (pp. 453–472). Malden, MA: Blackwell Publishing.

Porkorni, J. L., Worthington, C., & Jamison, P. (2004). Phonological awareness intervention: Comparison of Fast ForWord, Earobics, and LiPS. *Journal of Educational Research*, 97, 147–158.

President's Commission on Excellence in Special Education (2002). *A new era: Revitalizing special education for children and their families*. Washington, DC: ED Pubs.

Price, C. J., & McCrory, E. (2005). Functional brain imaging studies of skilled reading and developmental dyslexia. In M. J. Snowling & C. Hulme (Eds.), *The Science of Reading* (pp. 473–496). Oxford, UK: Blackwell Publishing.

Puolakanaho, A., Ahonen, T., Aro, M., Eklund, K., Leppanen, P. H. T., Poikkeus, A., Tolvanen, A., Torppa, M., & Lyytinen, H. (2007). Very early phonological and language skills: Estimating individual risk of reading disability. *Journal of Child Psychology & Psychiatry*, 48, 923–931.

Rack, J. P., Snowling, M. J., Hulme, C., & Gibbs, S. (2007). No evidence that an exercise-based treatment programme (DDAT) has specific benefits for children with reading difficulties. *Dyslexia*, 13, 97–104.

Raskind, W., Hsu, L., Thomson, J., Berninger, V., & Wijsman, E. (2000). Family aggregation of dyslexia phenotypes. *Behavioral Genetics*, 30, 385–396.

Rayner, K. (1978). Eye movements in reading and information processing. *Psychological Bulletin*, 85, 618–660.

Rayner, K. (1998). Eye movements in reading and information processing: Twenty years of research. *Psychological Bulletin*, 124, 372–422.

Reach Out and Read. (n.d.). *Developmental milestones of early literacy*. Retrieved December 17, 2007, from http://www.reachoutandreadsc.org/

Read, Write & Type! Research Results. (n.d.) The Writing Wagon Project. Retrieved September 17, 2003, from http://www.readwritetype.com/research_wagon.html

Reynolds, C. R. (1990). Conceptual and technical problems in learning disability diagnosis. In C. R. Reynolds & R. W. Kamphaus (Eds.), *Handbook of psychological and educational assessment of children: Intelligence and achievement* (pp. 127–165). New York: Guilford Press.

Richards, T. L., Aylward, E. H., Field, K. M., Gimme, A. C., Raskind, W., Richards, A. L., Nagy, W., Eckert, M., Leonard, C., Abbott, R. D., & Berninger, V. W. (2006). Converging evidence for triple word form theory in children with dyslexia. *Developmental Neuropsychology*, 30, 547–589.

Reynolds, C. R., & Kamphaus, R. W. (2004). Behavior assessment system for children (2nd ed.). Circle Pines, MN: American Guidance Service.

Reynolds, D., & Nicolson, R. I. (2006). Follow-up of an exercise-based treatment for children with reading difficulties. *Dyslexia*, 13, 78–96.

Reynolds, D., Nicolson, R. I., & Hambly, H. (2003). Evaluation of an exercise-based treatment for children with reading difficulties. *Dyslexia*, 9, 48–71.

Rieid, D., Hresko, W., & Hammill, D. D. (2004). *Test of Early Reading Ability –3*. Austin TX: Pro-Ed.

Roberts, J. E., Burchinal, M. K., Jackson, S. C., Hooper, S. R., Roush, J., Mundy, M., Neike, E. C., & Zeisel, S. A. (2000). Otitis medea in childhood in relation to preschool language and school readiness skills among black children. *Pediatrics*, 106, 725–735.

Roberts, J. E., Burchinal, M. R., & Zeisel, S. A. (2002). Otitis media in early childhood in relation to children's school-age language and academic skills. *Pediatrics*, 110, 696–716.

Roberts, R., & Mather, N. (1997). Orthographic dyslexia: The neglected subtype. *Learning Disabilities Research and Practice*, 12, 236–250.

Robinson, G., & Conway, R. (1990). The effects of Irlen colored lenses on students' specific reading skills and their perception of ability: A 12 month validity study. *Journal of Learning Disabilities*, 23, 589–596.

Rosner, J. (1974). Auditory analysis with pre-readers. *The Reading Teacher*, 27, 379–381.

Rosner, J. (1979). *Helping children overcome learning difficulties*. New York: Walker and Company.

Ross, S. M., Smith, L. J., & Casey, J. P. (1997). Preventing early school failure: Impacts of Success for All on standardized test outcomes, minority group performance, and school effectiveness. *Journal of Education for Students Placed At Risk*, 2(1), 29–53.

Roush, J. (2001). Screening for hearing loss and otitis medea: Basic principles. In J. Roush (Ed.), *Screening for hearing loss and otitis medea in children* (pp. 3–32) San Diego, CA: Singular.

Rutter, M., Caspi, A., Fergusson, D., Horwood, L. J., Goodman, R., Maughan, B., Moffitt, T., Meltzer, H., & Carroll, J. (2004). Sex differences in developmental reading disability: New findings from 4 epidemiological studies. *Journal of the American Medical Association*, 291, 2007–2012.

Ryan, M. (1994). *The other sixteen hours: The social and emotional problems of dyslexia*. Baltimore, MD: The International Dyslexia Association.

Sadoski, M., & Willson, V. L. (2006). Effects of a theoretically based large-scale reading intervention in a multicultural urban school district. *American Educational Research Journal*, 43, 137–154.

Scarborough, H. S. (1990). Very early language deficits in dyslexic children. *Child Development*, 61, 1728–1743.

Scarborough, H. S. (1991). Antecedents to reading disability: Preschool language development and literacy experiences of children with dyslexia. *Reading and Writing*, 3, 219–233.

Scarborough, H. S. (1998a). Early identification of children at risk for reading disabilities: Phonological awareness and some other promising predictors. In B. K. Shapiro, P. J. Accardo, & A. J. Capute (Eds.), *Specific reading disability: A view of the spectrum* (pp. 75–119). Timonium, MD: York Press.

Scarborough, H. S. (1998b). Predicting the future reading achievement of second graders with reading disabilities: Contributions of phonemic awareness, verbal memory, rapid serial naming and IQ. *Annals of Dyslexia*, 48, 115–136.

Scarborough, H. S. (2005). Developmental relationships between language and reading: Reconciling a beautiful hypothesis with some ugly facts. In H. W. Catts & A. G. Kamhi (Eds.), *The connections between language and reading disabilities* (pp. 3–24) Mahwah, NJ: Lawrence Erlbaum.

Scarborough, H. S., & Parker, J. D. (2003). Matthew effects in children with learning disabilities: Development of reading, IQ, and psychosocial problems from grade 2 to grade 8. *Annals of Dyslexia*, 53, 47–71.

Schatschneider, C., & Torgesen, J. K. (2004). Using our current understanding of dyslexia to support early identification and intervention. *Journal of Child Neurology*, 19, 759–770.

Scientific Learning Corporation. (1999). *Fast ForWord companion: A comprehensive guide to the training exercises*. Berkeley, CA: Author.

Semel, E., Wiig, E. H., & Secord, W. A. (2003). *Clinical Evaluation of Language Fundamentals* (4th ed.). San Antonio, TX: The Psychological Corporation/A Harcourt Assessment Company.

Shanahan, T. (2005). Review of DIBELS: Dynamic Indicators of Basic Early Literacy Skills, Sixth Edition. In R. A. Spies, & B. S. Plake, (Eds.). *The sixteenth mental measurements yearbook*. Lincoln, NE: Buros Institute of Mental Measurements.

Shankweiler, D., Crain, S., Katz, L., Fowler, A. E., Liberman, A. M., Brady, S. A., Thornton, R., Lundquist, E., Dreyer, L., Fletcher, J. M., Stuebing, K. K., Shaywitz, S. E., & Shaywitz, B. A. (1995). Cognitive profiles of reading disabled children: Comparison of language skills in phonology, morphology, and syntax. *Psychological Science*, 6, 149–156.

Shapiro, E. S. (2004). *Academic skills problems: Direct assessment and intervention* (3rd ed.). New York: Guilford Press.

Shatil, E., & Share, D. L. (2003). Cognitive antecedents of early reading ability: A test of the modularity hypothesis. *Journal of Experimental Child Psychology*, 86, 1–32.

Shaywitz, B. A., Fletcher, J. M., & Shaywitz, S. E. (1994). Issues in the definition and classification of attention deficit disorder. *Topics in Language Disorders*, 14, 1–25.

Shaywitz, B. A., Shaywitz, S. E., Blachman, B. A., Pugh, K. R., Fulbright, R. K., Skudlarski, P. et al (2004). Development of left occipitotemporal systems for skilled reading in children after a phonologically-based Intervention. *Biological Psychiatry*, 55, 926–933.

Shaywitz, S. (2003). *Overcoming dyslexia: A new and complete science-based program for reading problems of any level*. New York: Knopf.

Shaywitz, S. E. (2004a). *Clues to dyslexia from second grade on*. Retrieved December 17, 2007, from http://www.readingrockets.org/article/69

Shaywitz, S. E. (2004b). *Clues to dyslexia in early childhood*. Retrieved December 17, 2007, http://www.readingrockets.org/article/70

Shaywitz, S. E., Escobar, M. D., Shaywitz, B. A., Fletcher, J. M., & Makuch, R. (1992). Evidence that dyslexia may represent the lower tail of a normal distribution of reading ability. *New England Journal of Medicine*, 326, 145–150.

Shaywitz, S. E., & Shaywitz, B. A. (2004). Reading disability and the brain. *Educational Leadership*, 61(6), 6–11.

Shaywitz, S. E., Shaywitz, B. A., Fletcher, J. M., & Escobar, M. D. (1990). Prevalence of reading disability in boys and girls: Results of the Connecticut Longitudinal Study. *Journal of the American Medical Association*, 264, 998–1002.

Shelley-Tremblay, J., O'Brien, N., & Langhinrichsen-Rohling, J. (2007). Reading disability in adjudicated youth: Prevalence rates, current models, traditional and innovative treatments. *Aggression & Violent Behavior*, 12, 376–392.

Simos, P. G., Fletcher, J. M., Bergman, E., Breier, J. I., Foorman, B. R., Castillo, E. M., Davis, N., Fitzgerald, M., & Papanicolaou, A. C. (2002). Dyslexia- specific brain activation profile becomes normal following successful remedial training. *Neurology*, 58, 1203–1213.

Simos, P. G., Fletcher, J. M., Denton, C., Sarkari, S., Billingsley-Marshall, R., & Papanicolaou, A. C. (2006). Magnetic source imaging studies of dyslexia interventions. *Developmental Neuropsychology*, 30, 591–611.

Simos, P. G., Fletcher, J. M., Sarkari, S., Billingsley-Marshall, R., Denton, C. A., & Papanicolaou, A. C. (2007). Intensive instruction affects brain magnetic activity associated with oral word reading in children with persistent reading disabilities. *Journal of Learning Disabilities*, 40, 37–48.

Simpson, J., & Everatt, J. (2005). Reception class predictors of literacy skills. *British Journal of Educational Psychology*, 75, 171–188.

Slavin, R. E., & Madden, N. A. (1999). *Success for All: Roots and Wings: Summary of research on achievement outcomes*. Baltimore, MD: Center for Research on the Education of Students, Johns Hopkins University and Howard University.

Slavin, R. E., & Madden, N. A. (2000). Research on achievement outcomes of Success for All: A summary and response to critics. *Phi Delta Kappan*, 82(1), 38–40, 59–66.

Slavin, R. E., Madden, N. A., Karweit, N. L., Dolan, L., & Wasik, B. A. (1992). *Success for All: A relentless approach to prevention and early intervention in elementary schools*. Arlington, VA: Educational Research Service.

Slavin, R. E., Madden, N. A., Karweit, N. L., Livermon, B. J., & Dolan, L. (1990). Success for All: First-year outcomes of a comprehensive plan for reforming urban education. *American Educational Research Journal*, 27, 255–278.

Smith, L. F. (2003). Review of the Test of Early Reading Ability (3rd ed.). In B. S. Plake, J. C. Impara, & R. A. Spies (Eds.). *The fifteenth mental measurements yearbook*. Lincoln, NE: Buros Institute of Mental Measurements.

Smith, S. D., Kimberling, W. J., Pennington, B. F., & Lubs, H. A. (1983). Specific reading disability: Identification of an inherited form through linkage analysis. *Science*, 219, 1345–1347.

Snow, C. E., Burns, M. S., & Griffin, P. (Eds.), (1998). *Preventing reading difficulties in young children*. Washington, DC: National Academy Press.

Snowling, M. J. (2005). Literacy outcomes for children with oral language impairments: Developmental interactions between language skills and learning to read. In H. W. Catts & A.

G. Kamhi (Eds.), *The connections between language and reading disabilities* (pp. 55–76). Mahwah, NJ: Lawrence Erlbaum.

Snowling, M. J. (2006). Language skills and learning to read: The dyslexia spectrum. In M. J. Snowling & J. Stackhouse (Eds.), *Dyslexia, speech and language: A practitioner's handbook* (2nd ed., pp. 1–14). Chichester, West Sussex: Whurr Publishers.

Snowling, M. J., Gallagher, A., & Frith, U. (2003). Family risk of dyslexia is continuous: Individual differences in the precursors of reading skill. *Child Development*, 74, 358–373.

Sofie, C. A., & Riccio, C. A. (2002). A comparison of multiple methods for the identification of children with reading disabilities. *Journal of Learning Disabilities*, 35, 234–244.

Spafford, C. A., & Grosser, G. S. (2005). *Dyslexia and reading difficulties: Research and resource guide for working with all struggling readers* (2nd ed.). Boston: Pearson Education.

Spanish-speaking Primary Students Boost Reading Skills in an After-School Computer Program using Read, Write & Type. (n.d.). Retrieved February 24, 2008, from http://www.read-writetype.com/research/spanish.html

Speece, D. L. (2005). Hitting the moving target known as reading development: Some thoughts on screening children for secondary interventions. *Journal of Learning Disabilities*, 38, 487–493.

Spekman, N., Goldberg, R., & Herman, K. (1993). An exploration of risk and resilience in the lives of individuals with learning disabilities. *Learning Disabilities Research and Practice*, 8, 11–18.

Spring, C., & Davis, J. M. (1988). Relations of digit naming speed with three components of reading. *Applied Psycholinguistics*, 9, 315–334.

Spring, C., & Farmer, R. (1975). Perceptual span of poor readers. *Journal of Reading Behavior*, 7, 297–305.

Stackhouse, J. (2006). Speech and spelling difficulties: What to look for. In M. J. Snowling & J. Stackhouse (Eds.), *Dyslexia, speech and language: A practitioner's handbook* (2nd ed., pp. 15–35). Chichester, West Sussex: Whurr Publishers.

Stanovich, K. (1986). Matthews effects in reading: Some consequences of individual differences in acquiring literacy. *Reading Research Quarterly*, 21, 360–407.

Stanovich, K. E. (1988). Explaining the differences between the garden-variety poor readers: The Phonological core variable- difference model. *Journal of Learning Disabilities*, 22, 487–492.

Stanovich, K. (1993). The construct validity of discrepancy definitions of reading disability. In G. R. Lyon, D. B. Gray, & J. F. Kavanaugh (Eds.), *Better understanding learning disabilities: New views on research and their implications for education and public policies* (pp. 273–307). Baltimore: MD: Brookes Publishing.

Stanovich, K. E. (2005). The future of a mistake; Will discrepancy measurement continue to make the learning disabilities field a pseudoscience? *Learning Disability Quarterly*, 28, 103–105.

Stanovich, K., Cunningham, A. E., & Freeman, N. H. (1984). Relation between early reading acquisition and word decoding with and without context: A longitudinal study of first grade children. *Journal of Educational Psychology*, 76, 668–677.

Stanovich, K., & Siegel, L. S. (1994). Phenotypic performance profile of children with reading disabilities: A regression-based test of the phonological-core variable difference model. *Journal of Educational Psychology*, 86, 24–53.

Stanovich, K. E., West, R. F., & Harrison, M. R. (1995). Knowledge growth and maintenance across the life span: The role of print exposure. *Developmental Psychology*, 31, 811–816.

Satz, P., Raredin, D., & Ross, J. (1971). An evaluation of a theory of specific developmental dyslexia. *Child Development*, 42, 2009–2021.

Stein, J. F., & Talcott, J. B. (1999). The magnocellular theory of dyslexia. *Dyslexia*, 5, 59–78.

Stein, J., Talcott, J., & Witten, C. (2001). The sensorimotor basis of developmental dyslexia. In A. Fawcett (Ed.), *Dyslexia: Theory and good practice* (pp. 63–88). London: Whurr Publishers.

Stein, J. F., & Walsh, V. (1997). To see but not to read: The magnocellular theory of dyslexia. *Trends in Neuroscience*, 20, 147–152.

Stein, S. (2001). The neurobiology of reading difficulties. In M. Wolf (Ed.). *Dyslexia, Fluency in the Brain* (pp. 3–22). Timonium, MD: York Press.

Stevens, D. A. (2000). *Leveraging technology to improve test scores: A case study of low-income Hispanic students*. Paper presented at the International Conference on Learning with Technology, Temple University.

Stoner, J. C. (1991). Teaching at-risk students to read using specialized techniques in the regular classroom. *Reading and Writing: An Interdisciplinary Journal*, 3, 1.

Swanson, H. L., Trainin, G., Necoechea, D. M., & Hammill, D. D. (2003). Rapid naming, phonological awareness, and reading: "A meta-analysis of the correlational evidence". *Review of Educational Research*, 73, 407–440.

Tabors, P. O., & Snow, C. E. (2002). Young bilingual children and early literacy development. In S. B. Neuman & D. K. Dickinson (Eds.), *Handbook of early literacy research* (pp. 159–178). New York: The Guilford press.

Talcott, J. B., Hansen, P. C., Willis-Owen, C., McKinnell, I. W., Richardson, A. J., & Stein, J. F. (1998). Visual magnocellular impairment in adult development dyslexics. *Neuro-Ophthalmology*, 20, 187–201.

Tallal, P. (1980). Auditory temporal perception, phonics, and reading disabilities in children. *Brain and Language*, 9, 182–198.

Tallal, P., Miller, S. C., & Fitch, R. (1993). Neurobiological basis of speech: A case for the preeminence of temporal processing. *Annals of the New York Academy of Sciences*, 682, 27–47.

Tallal, P., Miller, S. L., Bedi, G., Byma, G., Wang, X., Nagarajan, S. S., Schreiner, C., Jenkins, W., & Merzenich, M. R. (1996). Language comprehension in language-learning impaired children improved with acoustically modified speech. *Science*, 271, 81–84.

Taylor, B., Pearson, P. D., Clark, K., & Walpole, S. (2000). Effective schools and accomplished teachers: Lessons about primary grade reading instruction in low income schools. *Elementary School Journal*, 101, 121–166.

Taylor, S. E. (1965). Eye movements in reading: Facts and fallacies. *American Educational Research Journal*, 2, 187–202.

Teeter, P. A., & Semrud-Clikeman, M. (1997). *Child neuropsychology: Assessment and interventions for neurodevelopmental disorders*. Needham Heights, MA: Allyn & Bacon.

Temple, E., Poldrack, R., Protopapas, A., Nagarajan, S., Salz, T., Tallal, P. M. M., Merzenich, M. M., & Gabrieli, J. D. E. (2000). Disruption of the neural response to rapid acoustic stimuli in dyslexia: Evidence from functional MRI. *Proceedings of the National Academy of Science*, 97, 13907–13912.

The Help Group. (n.d.). *Early warning signs of dyslexia*. Retrieved December 17, 2007, http://www.thehelpgroup.org/pdf/ewsigns_dyslexia.pdf

Tivnan, T., & Hemphill, L. (2004). Comparing literacy reform models in high poverty schools: Patterns of first grade achievement. *The Elementary School Journal*, 105, 419–442.

Tomatis, A. (1978). *Education and dyslexia*. France-Quebec: Les Editions.

Torgesen, J. K. (1995). *Phonological awareness: A critical factor in dyslexia*. Baltimore, MD: The International Dyslexia Association.

Torgesen, J. K. (2002a). Lessons learned from intervention research in reading: A way to go before we rest. In R. Stanhope (Ed.) *Learning and teaching reading* (Vol. 1, pp. 89–103). London: British Psychological Society.

Torgesen, J. K. (2002b). The prevention of reading difficulties. *Journal of School Psychology*, 40, 7–27.

Torgesen, J. K. (2004). Lessons learned from research on interventions for students who have difficulty learning to read. In V. P. C. McCardle (Ed.), *The voice of evidence in reading research* (pp. 355–382). Baltimore, MD: Paul Brooks.

Torgesen, J. K. (2006). *The full Power 4 Kids report*. (pp. IX–109). Retrieved January 22, 2008, from http://www.haan4kids.org/power4kids/

Torgesen, J. K., Alexander, A. W., Wagner, R. K., Rashotte, C. A., Voeller, K. S., & Conway, T. (2001). Intensive remedial instruction for children with severe reading disabilities: Immediate and long-term outcomes from two instructional approaches. *Journal of Learning Disabilities*, 34, 33–58.

Torgesen, J. K., & Bryant, P. E. (2004). *Test of Phonological Awareness – Second Edition: PLUS.* Austin TX: Pro-Ed.

Torgesen, J. K., & Houck, D. (1980). Processing deficiencies of learning-disabled children who perform poorly on the digit span test. *Journal of Educational Psychology*, 72, 141–160.

Torgesen, J. K., Rashotte, C. A., & Alexander, A. W. (2001). Principles of fluency instruction in reading: Relationships with established empirical outcomes. In M. Wolf (Ed.), *Dyslexia, fluency, and the brain* (pp. 333–356). Timonium, MD: York Press.

Torgesen, J. K., & Wagner, R. K. (1994). Longitudinal studies of phonological processing and reading. *Journal of Learning Disabilities*, 27, 276.

Torgesen, J. K., Wagner, R. K., & Rashotte, C. A. (1997). Prevention and remediation of severe reading disabilities: Keeping the end in mind. *Scientific Studies of Reading*, 1, 217–234.

Torgesen, J. K., Wagner, R. K., & Rashotte, C. A. (1999). *Test of Word Reading Efficiency.* Austin, TX: Pro-Ed.

Torgesen, J. K., Wagner, R. K., Rashotte, C. A., Burgess, S., & Hecht, S. (1997). Contributions of phonological awareness and rapid automatic naming ability to the growth of word-reading skills in second-to-fifth-grade children. *Scientific Studies of Reading*, 1(2), 161–185.

Torgesen, J. K., Wagner, R. K., Rashotte, C. A., & Herron, J. (n.d.). *Summary of outcomes from first grade study with Read, Write, and Type and Auditory Discrimination in Depth instruction and software with at-risk children. (Tech. Rep. No. 2).* Tallahassee, Fl: Florida State University, Department of Psychology.

Torgesen, J. K., Wagner, R. K., Rashotte, C. A., Rose, E., Lindamood, P., Conway, T., & Garvan, C. (1999). Preventing reading failure in young children with phonological processing disabilities: Group and individual responses to instruction. *Journal of Educational Psychology*, 91, 579–593.

Tunick, R. A., & Pennington, B. F. (2002). The etiological relationship between reading disability and phonological disorder. *Annals of Dyslexia*, 52, 75–97.

U.S. Department of Education. (2006). 34 CFR: Assistance to states for the education of children with disabilities and preschool grants for children with disabilities. Final rules. *Federal Register*, 71, 46540–46845.

U.S. Department of Education. (2007, April 19). *Reading First achievement data demonstrate dramatic improvements in reading proficiency of America's neediest children: State-by-state data confirm that the scientifically based reading program is working.* Retrieved December 10, 2007, from http://www.ed.gov/news/pressreleases/2007/04/04192007.html

U.S. Department of Education. (2007). Response to intervention and early intervening services. Washington, DC: Author. Retrieved February 23, 2008, from http://idea.ed.gov/explore/view/p/%2Croot%2Cdynamic%2CPresentation%2C28%2C

U.S. Department of Education, Of Special Education and Rehabilitative Services. (2002). *A new era: Revitalizing special education for children and their families.* Washington, DC: Author.

U.S. Department of Education, Office of Special Education and Rehabilitative Services, Office of Special Education (2007). *27th Annual (2005) Report to Congress on the Implementation of the Individuals with Disabilities Education Act.* Washington, DC: Author. Retrieved from http://www.ed.gov/about/reports/annual/osep/2005/index.html

Uhry, J. K., & Clark, D. B. (2004). *Dyslexia: Theory and practice of instruction* (3rd ed.). Austin, TX: Pro-Ed.

Vaughn, S., & Fuchs, L. S. (2003). Redefining learning disabilities as inadequate response to instruction: The promise and potential problems. *Learning Disabilities Research & Practice*, 18, 137–146.

Vellutino, F. R. (1979). Dyslexia: *Theory and research. Cambridge*, MA: MIT press.

Vellutino, F. R., Fletcher, J. M., Snowling, M. J., & Scanlon, D. M. (2004). Specific reading disability (dyslexia): What have we learned in the past four decades? *Journal of Child Psychology and Psychiatry*, 45, 2–40.

Vellutino, F. R., Scanlon, D. M., Small, S., & Fanuele, D. P. (2006). Response to intervention as a vehicle for distinguishing between children with and without reading disabilities: Evidence for the role of kindergarten and first-grade interventions. *Journal of Learning Disabilities*, 39, 157–169.

Vellutino, F. R., Scanlon, D. M., & Tanzman, M. S. (1994). Components of reading ability: Issues and problems in operationalizing word identification, phonological coding, and orthographic coding. In G. R. Lyon (Ed.), *Frames of reference for the assessment of learning disabilities: New views on measurement issues* (pp. 279–324). Baltimore, MD: Paul H. Brookes.

Vellutino, F. R., Tunmer, W. E., Jaccard, J. J., & Chen, R. (2007). Components of reading ability: Multivariate evidence for a convergent skills model of reading development. *Scientific Studies of Reading*, 11, 3–32.

Vitale, M., Medland, M., Romance, N., & Weaver, H. P. (1993). Accelerating reading and thinking skills of low-achieving elementary students. Implications for curricular change. *Effective School Practices*, 1, 26–31.

Voeller, K. K. S. (2004). Dyslexia. *Journal of Child Neurology*, 19, 740–744.

Waber, D. (2001). Aberrations in timing in children with impaired reading. In M. Wolf (Ed.), *Dyslexia, fluency and the brain* (pp. 103–128). Timonium, MD: York Press.

Wadsworth, S. J., Defries, J. C., Stevenson, J., Gilger, J. W., & Pennington, P. F. (1992). Gender ratios among reading disabled children and their siblings as a function of parental impairment. *Journal of Child Psychology and Psychiatry*, 33, 1229–1239.

Wadsworth, S. J., Olson, R. K., Pennington, B. F., & DeFries, J. C. (2000). Differential genetic etiology of reading disability as a function of IQ. *Journal of Learning Disabilities*, 33, 192–200.

Wagner, R. K., & Torgesen, J. K. (1987). The nature of phonological processing and its causal role in the acquisition of reading skills. *Psychological Bulletin*, 101, 192–212.

Wagner, R. K., Torgesen, J. K., & Rashotte, C. A. (1999). *Comprehensive Test of Phonological Processing*. Austin, TX: Pro-Ed.

Wagner, R. K., Torgesen, J. K., Rashotte, C. A., Hecht, S. A., Barker, T. A., Burgess, S. R.,Donahue, J., & Garon, T. (1997). Changing relations between phonological processing abilities and word-level reading as children develop from beginning to skilled readers: A 5-year longitudinal study. *Developmental Psychology*, 33, 468–479.

Wallace, I. F., & Hooper, S. R. (1997). Otitis medea and its impact on cognition, academic, and behavioral outcomes: A review and interpretation of the findings. In J. E. Roberts, I. F. Wallace, & F. Henderson (Eds.), *Otitis medea, language and learning in young children: Medical, developmental and educational considerations* (pp. 173–194). Baltimore: Brookes.

Walley, A. (1993). The role of vocabulary development in children's spoken word recognition and segmentation ability. *Developmental Review*, 13, 286–350.

Ward, A. M. (2003). Review of the Phonological Abilities Test. In B. S. Plake, J. C. Impara, & R. A. Spies (Eds.). *The fifteenth mental measurements yearbook*. Lincoln, NE: Buros Institute of Mental Measurements.

Weiderhold, L., & Blalock . (2000). *Gray Silent Reading Test*. Austin TX: Pro-Ed.

Weiderhold, L., & Bryant, B. (2001). *Gray Oral Reading Test* (4th ed.). Austin TX: Pro-Ed.

Wilde, J., Goerss, B., & Wesler, J. (2003). Are all phonemic awareness tests created equally? A comparison of the Yopp-Singer and the task of auditory analysis skills (TASS). *Journal of Research in Reading*, 26, 295–304.

Wilkins, M., & Garside, A. H. (1993). *Basic facts about dyslexia: What every lay person ought to know*. Baltimore, MD: Interactional Dyslexia Association.

Willcutt, E. G., & Pennington, B. F. (2000a). Comorbidity of reading disability and attention-deficit/hyperactivity disorder: Differences by gender and subtype. *Journal of Learning Disabilities*, 33, 179–191.

Willcutt, E. G., & Pennington, B. F. (2000b). Psychiatric comorbidity in children and adolescents with reading disability. *Journal of Child Psychology and Psychiatry*, 41, 1039–1048.

Willcutt, E. G., Pennington, B. F., & DeFries, J. C. (2000). A twin study of the etiology of co-morbidity between reading disability and attention-deficit/hyperactivity disorder. *American Journal of Medical Genetics (Neuropsychiatric Genetics)*, 96, 293–301.

Willcutt, E. G., Pennington, B. F., Smith, S. D., Cardon, L. R., Gayan, J., Knopik, V. S., Olson, R. K., & DeFries, J. C. (2002). Quantitative trait locus for reading disability on chromosome 6p is pleiotropic for attention-deficit/hyperactivity disorder. *American Journal of Medical Genetics: Neuropsychiatric Genetics*, 114, 260–268.

Wilson, B. A. (1988a). *Instructors manual*. Millbury, MA: Wilson Language Training.

Wilson, B. A. (1988b). *Wilson reading system program overview*. Millbury, MA: Wilson Language Training.

Wilson, B. A. (2002). *The Wilson Reading System* (3rd ed.). Oxford, MA: Wilson Language Training.

Wilson, B. A., & O'Connor, J. R. (1995). Effectiveness of the Wilson Reading System used in public school training. In C. McIntyre & J. Pickering (Eds.), *Clinical studies of multisensory structured language education* (pp. 247–254). Salem, OR: International Multisensory Structured Language Education Council.

Wilson, B. A., & Schupack, H. (1997). *Reading, writing and spelling- The multisensory structured language approach*. Baltimore, MD: The International Dyslexia Association.

Wilson, M. S., & Reschley, D. J. (1996). Assessment in school psychology training and practice. *School Psychology Review*, 25, 9–23.

Winskel, H. (2006). The effects of an early history of otitis media on children's language and literacy skill development. *British Journal of Educational Psychology*, 76, 727–744.

Witelson, S. F. (1976). Sex and the single hemisphere: Right hemisphere specialization for spatial processing. *Science*, 193, 425–427.

Witelson, S. F., & Robinovitch, M. S. (1972). Hemispheric speech lateralization in children with auditory-linguistic deficits. *Cortex*, 8, 412–426.

Wolf, M. (1991). Naming speed and reading: the contribution of the cognitive neurosciences. *Reading Research Quarterly*, 26, 123–140.

Wolf, M. (2001). Seven dimensions of time. In M. Wolfe (Ed.), *Dyslexia, fluency and the brain* (pp. ix–xix). Timonium, MD: York Press.

Wolf, M., & Bowers, P. (1999). The "double-deficit hypothesis" for the developmental dyslexias. *Journal of Educational Psychology*, 91, 1–24.

Wolf, M., Bowers, P., & Biddle, K. (2000). Naming-speed processes, timing, and reading: A conceptual review. *Journal of Learning Disabilities*, 33, 387–408.

Wolf, M., & Obergon, M. (1992). Early naming deficits, developmental dyslexia, and a specific deficit hypothesis. *Brain and Language*, 42, 219–247.

Wood, F. (2002). *Data analysis of the Wilson Reading System*. Retrieved February 23, 2008, from http://www.wilsonlanguage.com/PDF/Evidence_Data_Analysis.pdf

Woodcock, R., McGrew, K., & Mather, N. (2001). *Woodcock Johnson Tests of Achievement*. (3rd ed.). Itasca, IL: Riverside Publishing.

Woodcock, R., Mather, N., & Schrank, F. (2007). *Woodcock-Johnson Diagnostic Reading Battery III*. Itasca IL: Riverside Publishing.

Yopp, H. K. (1995). A test for assessing phonemic awareness in young children. *Reading Teacher*, 49, 20–30.

Ziegler, J. C., & Goswami, U. (2005). Reading acquisition, developmental dyslexia, and skilled reading across languages: A psycholinguistic grain size theory. *Psychological Bulletin*, 131, 3–29.

Zimmerman, T. (2004). The effects of visualization instruction on first graders story retelling. In J. A. E. Dugan, P. E. Linder, M. B. Sampson, B. A. Brancato, & L. Elish-Piper (Eds.), *Celebrating the power of literacy* (pp. 67–77). Pittsburg: KS: College Reading Association.

Index

Lightning Source UK Ltd.
Milton Keynes UK
13 November 2009

146189UK00009B/160/P